The Romantic Tradition in American Literature

The Romantic Tradition in American Literature

Advisory Editor

HAROLD BLOOM
Professor of English, Yale University

VIRGINALIA;

OR,

SONGS OF MY SUMMER NIGHTS

A Gift of Love for the Beautiful

T[HOMAS] H[OLLEY] CHIVERS

ARNO PRESS

A NEW YORK TIMES COMPANY
New York • 1972

Reprint Edition 1972 by Arno Press Inc.

Reprinted from a copy in The Emory
University Library

The Romantic Tradition in American Literature
ISBN for complete set: 0-405-04620-0
See last pages of this volume for titles.

Manufactured in the United States of America

೧೭೦೩೦೩೦೩೦೩೦೩೦೩೦೩೦

Library of Congress Cataloging in Publication Data

Chivers, Thomas Holley, 1809-1858.
    Virginalia.

    (The Romantic tradition in American literature)
    I. Title. II. Series.
PS1294.C4V5 1972   811'.3   72-4958
ISBN 0-405-04630-8

VIRGINALIA

VIRGINALIA

SONGS OF MY SUMMER NIGHTS

THOMAS HOLLEY CHIVERS

RESEARCH CLASSICS No. 2 1942

The original edition of "Virginalia" was lent through the courtesy of the American Antiquarian Society.

Twelve leaves of advertisements bound in at the end of the original book have been omitted from this reprint.

This edition has been enlarged 10% in order to make the annotations in diamond type (4½ points) more legible.

MANUFACTURED IN THE U. S. A.

COPYRIGHT 1942 BY EUGENE L. SCHWAAB

3124 AVENUE J   BROOKLYN, NEW YORK

THOMAS HOLLEY CHIVERS, 1809-1858

It is a commonplace that a poet's talent is not always appraised correctly by his contemporaries. Yet the later critic must, view him in his contemporary surroundings in order to get the proper perspective for evaluating his work. Critical inaccuracies are compounded in the casuality of an incompetent reviewer or in the heat of a controversy in which judiciousness has been consumed. Such inaccuracies are perpetuated into myths when succeeding critics neglect independently to investigate sources, or when the source material is not readily available. It is to remedy the latter situation that this reprint is made available.

Chivers did not have a fair hearing in his lifetime. He lived in a magazine age when editors cordially encouraged their readers to contribute verse and, worse yet, printed most of it. Yet the same editors not merely offered no encouragement to Chivers, but publicly rejected his proffered contributions with loud columnar guffaws. As a southerner, probably the greatest ignominy that Chivers had to endure was his complete rejection by the South's great arbiter of belles lettres — the *Southern Literary Messenger*. His first offer in 1835 was rejected (perhaps by the then editor Poe) with scorn and the next and last editorial notice taken of him was in 1853 when an anonymous predecessor of Bayard Taylor derided his "Atlanta" for two full pages. Even his native Georgian "Orion" scandalized his name. The plagiarism controversy with Poe represented the height of critical notice that Chivers ever received. After his death in 1858 his name entered the literary scene only vis-à-vis Poe — and then chiefly at the instigation of the detractors of Poe rather than because of any esteem for Chivers.

In his lifetime, with the exception of Poe, no literary critic took his work seriously. One reason was that while all writers turn out some minor work, Chivers' percentage was unusually high both in quantity and quality. When the effect he strove to attain did not come off, it was not just poor verse — it was ludicrous or even unintelligible. On the other hand, his audience was too undeveloped to understand what his poetic aims were, so that even when he succeeded in striking the desired note, his audience was not attuned. Lacking a competent criticism from professional critics and an esthetically developed public that could guide him in his experiments, he was thrown back on his own devices. Alone he could not control or modulate, except here and there, the wild song that came to his lips. Alone he never attained the pinnacle to which he aspired and no help was forthcoming from his environment.

Yet this is only part of the explanation for his failure — actually it is a familiar symptom, rather than the cause. The *cause* is the one which evoked similar manifestations of frustration from Poe, Melville, Margaret Fuller and others. Diverse reasons can be given in each individual case as contributory to the cause, but basically the failure lay in an inadequate personal integration with contemporary American life.

That is the position in which Chivers found himself. Oppressed by misfortune in his personal life, he had no perspective and became maudlin and unintelligible in his grief. His family and friends were inadequate intellectual companions, he wandered alone and pre-occupied with his personal affairs. Unable to come to terms with the world of reality, his visions and the world of spiritualism became the world in which he dwelt. He wrote of himself to himself, grew ever more ingrown, and his poetry reflected this process. Under such self-imposed disadvantageous circumstances he was experimenting with original poetic forms — a difficult task under the best of circumstances and it is surprising that more often than not success attended his efforts.

Thus he went his restless, lonely way. A Southerner, he lived much in the North, yet never took root there. Fortunately for him, he was a man of some wealth, and insofar as money could alleviate his situation, it was available. He did not suffer any material discomforts as did his contemporary Poe. His means also enabled him to publish his volumes of verse out of his own pocket. Almost without exception the successive volumes thus issued were either ignored or ridiculed. As might be surmised every one of his books is now rare.

Since the few copies that exist are naturally in the rare book rooms of a few libraries, this reprint is intended to make Chivers' work more easily available to the research worker. At the same time it affords the undergraduate student and lay reader the opportunity of becoming acquainted with Chivers' poetry by giving him a volume he can carry in his pocket and browse in at will. "VIRGINALIA" was chosen because it represents more of the best of Chivers than any other single volume.

It is to be hoped that the present reprint will create sufficient interest to justify the preparation of a definitive edition of the complete works of Dr. Chivers by some university or foundation.

Dr. THOMAS HOLLEY CHIVERS, of New York, is at the same time one of the best and one of the worst poets in América. His productions affect one as a wild dream — strange, incongruous, full of images of more than arabesque monstrosity, and snatches of sweet unsustained song. Even his worst nonsense (and some of it is horrible) has an indefinite charm of sentiment and melody. We can never be sure that there is *any* meaning in his words — neither is there any meaning in many of our finest musical airs — but the effect is very similar in both. His figures of speech are metaphor run mad, and his grammar is often none at all. Yet there are as fine individual passages to be found in the poems of Dr. Chivers, as in those of any poet whatsoever.

Edgar Allan Poe in Graham's Magazine, Dec. 1841

VIRGINALIA;

OR,

SONGS OF MY SUMMER NIGHTS.

A Gift of Love for the Beautiful.

BY T. H. CHIVERS, M. D.

"Αυτο καθ' αυτο μεθ' αυτου, μονο ειδες αιει ον." — *Plato.*

PHILADELPHIA:

LIPPINCOTT, GRAMBO & CO.

1853.

PRESS OF THE
FRANKLIN PRINTING HOUSE,
No. 210 Washington Street,
BOSTON.

PREFACE.

———

THAT Diamond whose peculiar mode of cutting causes
it to give out, or reveal, the richest amount of acromatic,
fiery lustre, is called *The Brilliant*. Now, this peculiar
gem consists in its being two truncated pyramids united
by a common base—the upper pyramid being much more
deeply truncated than the lower one. This beautiful, as
well as very remarkable jewel, consists of a crown, girdle
and collet—the crown amounting to one-third and the
collet to two-thirds of the whole height of the gem. The
table and collet are regular octagons, and the facets
occupied by the bisel, (which is that space lying between
the girdle and table,) are eight lozenges, with twenty-four
triangles, and are called star-facets—the English double
Brilliant consisting of twenty-four facets, table and collet,
sixteen of which terminate in the form of a star in the
bisel.

Now, you may as well tell me that a rough Diamond,
newly dug out of the mines in Golconda, can be made the
Mediator of the revelation of as much purely white light
from the sun, as one that has been anointed to the office
by the ingenuity of the Lapidary, as to tell me that any
Poem can become the mediation of the revelation of the
influx of the Divine Life of God into the soul, without the

highest knowledge of the true Art of musical language in the Poet—for just as the first owes its ability to express itself crystallinely to the peculiar mode of that cutting which is best calculated, according to the highest mathematical laws appertaining to the full development of light through a multiplication of highly polished facets—so does a full manifestation, or Shekinization, of the passions and emotions of the soul depend entirely upon the Art displayed in its creation, according to certain musical laws, by the Poet.

Now, as a Brilliant, by having the facets on the bisel and collet side thrice cut, has its value increased, because it is, thereby, enabled to give out a greater amount of white light, so is a Poem more beautiful and captivating to the soul which has the highest passion revealed through the loftiest Art—for a Brilliant, of one carat, whose planes and faces bear legitimate proportions to the pyramidal height and breadth of its truncation, is worth twice as much as an uncut diamond of equal weight—because, under such conditions, it is rendered capable of revealing the greatest amount of crystal fire. For as the Diamond is the crystalline Revelator of the acromatic white light of Heaven, so is a perfect Poem the crystalline revelation of the Divine Idea. There is just the difference between a pure Poem and one that is not, that there is between the spiritual concretion of a Diamond and the mere glaciation of water into ice. For as the irradiency of a Diamond depends upon its diaphanous translucency, so does the beauty of a Poem upon its rhythmical crystalization of the Divine Idea.

Now, in regard to the Refrain of a Poem, I would merely mention here, that it is not only an ornament, but an essence—a life—a vitality—an immortal soul—not a mere profane appendage, but a sacred Symbolical Ensignium— a crown of beauty, and a diamond of glory, like the Urim and Thummim on the Breastplate of the High Priest—or, those beautiful golden bells which jeweled the hem of his garment—making a pleasant chime. It is to a Poem precisely what Ovid says of the outward golden tire of the many-spoked wheels of the Chariot of Apollo, that makes a continual, ever-recurring Auroral chime at every revolution of the wheels, proportionate to their velocity, which is never lost, or dies away into at echo, but forever returns upon itself, like the menstrual changes of the Moon, but only to be made the same sweet Moon—the same sweet Auroral chime.

It is, therefore, obvious that no true Poet ever yet wrote for the Aristarchi of the world—only to show them how little they know—but only for the divine Areopagus of Heaven. How can the mere Critic judge of that which belongs only to the Artist? That which is New cannot be deciphered by the Old. The Sphinx-Riddle cannot be solved by any Œdipus this side of the Nile. Old ears cannot hear New Music; old eyes cannot see New Visions; nor can Old Tongues taste of the delicious white-wine of Heaven.

Thus have I moulded on the swift-circling wheel of my soul some of the manifold members of that Divine Beauty which lives immortal in the shining House of Life.

T. H. C.

Boston, December 15th, 1852.

INDEX.

VIRGINALIA;

OR,

SONGS OF MY SUMMER NIGHTS.

CHACTAS;

OR,

THE LAMENT OF THE HARMONIOUS VOICE.

Founded on Chataubriande's Atala.

It will be now, the next Moon of young flowers,
Just seven-times-ten long snows of rushing hours,
With four Moons more, since mother gave me birth,
And raised me up to wander on this earth.
Nursed in the wind-rocked cradle of the beach,
I grew unharmed above the Panther's reach—
Beneath the Mighty Oaks whose stately ranks
Now bristle on the Muschecheebee's* banks.
But fatal, fatal, fatal was the day
When Chactas came from Pensacola Bay!

I was but sixteen fallings of the leaf,
When Outalissa, son of Miscou, Chief
In Cuscovilla's Valley, went to war
Against the Muscogulgees from afar—
When, on the mighty River of Mobile,
My father fell beneath an Outcast's steel!

* The Mississippi.

2

The Thunders echoed to his dying groan,
Responsive to the echoes of mine own!
For fatal, fatal, fatal was the day
When Chactas came from Pensacola Bay!

But so Areskou* willed it from the sky,
Though it was hard for me to see him die!
And they had nearly torn me limb from limb,
As by his side I stood defending him—
(Would that mine own had followed him where rolls
The mighty River to the Land of Souls!)—
But then they made me captive in the fight,
And bound me in their wigwam all the night!
Ah! fatal, fatal, fatal was the day
When Chactas came from Pensacola Bay!

Then it was thought that we were doomed to go
And tend the Silver-Mines of Mexico;
But Lopez, a Castillian, who was kind,
Persuaded them to let me stay behind.
Moved by my youth, (then scarcely seventeen,)
He took me home with him to Augustine.
But after thirty Moons were spent with him,
My health declined—my very eyes grew dim!
But fatal, fatal, fatal was the day
When Chactas came from Pensacola Bay.

And though he often urged me to remain,
I longed to see my native land again.
"Alas! then, Child of Nature! go," said he,
"Where some remembrances were left by me!"
And saying this, he took me by the hand,
And bade me farewell for my native land.

* The God of War.

But when he said that we should meet no more,
I never felt so sorrowful before!
For fatal, fatal, fatal was the day
When Chactas left old Pensacola Bay.

But ere my feet had touched my native sod,
Because I had refused to worship God—
(As Lopez had foretold me on that day—)
The Muscogulgees caught me by the way,
And bound me, in the midst of all my grief,
And took me back to Simighan, their Chief,
Who called aloud to me to speak my name?
I TOLD him, "CHACTAS!" "CHACTAS! 'tis the same!"
Ah! fatal, fatal, fatal was the day
When Chactas came from Pensacola Bay!

"The Son of OUTALISSA?"   "*Thou should'st know,*"
I said, then pointed to my Locust Bow.
"*See you this dress—these feathers on my head?*
I am his son.   The Nation's CHIEF *is dead!*"
And then, as if made frantic with delight,
He said, "*Rejoice! for thou shalt die to-night!*"
I knew that all was over with me then,
And Hope should never visit me again!
Ah! fatal, fatal, fatal was the day
When Chactas came from Pensacola Bay!

I knew, from that sad hour, that but to die
Was all my portion—yet, made no reply.
And as they bore me through the mighty throng,
I chaunted out aloud mine own Death-Song!
And then they bound me to an old Oak Tree,
On Apalachachulee by the sea,
And built around me my funeral Pile,
Making their Warriors watch me all the while!
Ah! fatal, fatal, fatal was the day
When Chactas came from Pensacola Bay!

And when the Virgins saw my wretched state,
They mourned, as women always do, my fate !
And asked me, when they wished my heart to prove,
" *If aught had ever whispered me of love ?*
If ever, on the green banks of the streams,
I had beheld the young Hind in my dreams ? "
I then replied, " *The Flowers love not the dew*
With half the tenderness I feel for you ! "
But fatal, fatal, fatal was the day
When Chactas came from Pensacola Bay !

" You have the MAGIC WORDS to cancel pain,
And though we part, yet we shall meet again ! "
Pleased with my flattery, they then gave to me
A Bowl of Syrup from the Maple-tree.
And when I told them I was doomed to die—
Through fiery flames to soar to Heaven on high !
They sighed in sorrow for my tender years,
And stood, lamenting by my couch, in tears !
Ah ! fatal, fatal, fatal was the day
When Chactas left old Pensacola Bay !

The night arrived. The pale Moon seemed to glide,
Weeping through Heaven, like Sorrow by my side—
When, lo ! before me, swaying down the grass,
A Maiden, beautiful as Heaven, did pass,
With noiseless steps, upon the silver sands,—
Then, turning round, untied my fettered hands !
It was CELUTA ! *Angel of my heart !*
With whom, rejoicing, I did then depart !.
For blessed, blessed, blessed was the day
When Chactas came from Pensacola Bay.

VILLA ALLEGRA, GA., July 10, 1839.

UNA;

OR,

THE LOST ONE.

Her beauty, like the Churches, shone afar,
　　The dark Earth with her presence ever whitening;
She looked upon me like the Evening Star
　　Upon the Earth, with eyes forever brightening
In the keen burning gladness of their own pure lightning.

Her rich cascade of loosely pouring hair
　　Around her Swan-white neck like lilies blowing,
In wavy gold broke on her bosom bare
　　In billowy ringlets—then, more stream-like growing,
Over her shoulders, prone, down to her feet went flowing.

Like some bright Angel out of Paradise,
　　With passionate lightnings full of mildest splendor,
Her soul looked through the Heaven of her blue eyes,
　　Subdued, like Violets by the dew, to render
Their heart-dissolving looks, thereby, more heavenly tender.

Her soft, voluptuous Aphroditean limbs
　　Were clothed with beauty as the Moon with splendor—
Which, like the Harmonies of heavenly Hymns
　　Swelling from Angel's lips to shapes most tender—
Their soft, impassioned movement seemed with grace to render

The air around all warmly musical—
　　Dissolving, silently, the Heavens above her,
Like an incarnate Moon majestical—
　　As if the soul was music that did move her,
And, Pleiad-like, could bring the Gods from Heaven to love her.

And thus she lived an Exile out of Heaven,
　　Ever expecting to return as surely
As if she knew that God had only given
　　Her life to try her if she could live purely—
The only way that she could Heaven possess securely.

2*

For she looked ever thence, as if she knew
    Heaven was her Home—forevermore imploring,
In acts all grateful unto me as dew
    To the parched flowers—(from grief my soul restoring)—
Her God to take her back with songs of pure adoring.

She ruled my soul with her mild regent will,
    As does the Moon the Sea with influences—
As queenlike as if she were sitting still
    In Heaven, upon the highest seat, in trances
Of rapture, listening to the Angel-excellences.

A golden stream of purest Poetry
    Flowed from her lips in Pythian inspiration—
Storming my heart, with its deep melody,
    To love immortal as her jubilation—
Which ruled my thoughts within as God rules the creation.

Her eyes were like two Violets bathed in dew,
    Upon one lily-bed, now close together,
As if just melted out of Heaven's own blue,
    Wherein two stars, unmelted, burned, or, rather,
Sparkled, which made them look like rain in fairest weather.

An incarnation of immortal Day,
    Forever cloudless, yet, forever raining—
Whose heart in its own love did melt away—
    Making her look like Happiness complaining
Of her own joy—too great for her pure soul's sustaining.

An incarnation of immortal love,
    Forever happy, yet, forever weeping,—
Glad that she was God's Angel from above,
    But wept that she was, through her body, keeping
The dark world bright, when she should Heaven above be reaping.

Out of the lutestrings of her heart she wove,
    Like Israfel in Heaven, with her sweet singing,
A subtle web of Poesy, which Love
    Around my heart then wound, wherewith, upspringing,
She to the Mount of Fame her way with me went winging.

Then, from their rosy nest in her pure heart,
    Her snow-white, dove-winged thoughts to Heaven went
        soaring—
Climbing, with unpremeditated Art,
    From star to star, up to the sun, downpouring
A deluge of deep song with Angel-like adoring.

Then, as the young Moon wanes into the night,
    Leaving all dark that was before enshrouded
In soft, diaphanous, Angel-vesture, white—
    So did her dying song leave me enclouded
In the dark night of grief, which then my heart encrowded!

—✧—

GANYMEDE.*

A little boy, with deep blue eyes
Flashing the glory of the skies—
With fair round cheeks, an only son,
Made ruddy by the Southern Sun—
Saw, from the verdant Vale below,
A Mountain in the morning glow,
Covered with everlasting snow—
Far up upon whose rocky height,
Exulting in the morning light,
Like Breastplate upon Aaron's breast,
Full towering over all the rest,

* Founded on an actual occurrence.

Which gave new glory to the Sun—
The glorious name of Washington!
While under it, shone from afar,
With glory like the Morning Star—
The glorious name—AMERICA!

Thus stood he in the Vale below,
Looking upon that Mountain's brow,
Like God's great Prophet, when he stood,
Burdened with Heaven, by Chebar flood—
Seeing this high-uplifted name
Burning upon the Mount of Fame,
There looked out of his deep blue eyes,
Flashing the glory of the skies—
The glorious hope that cannot die—
The light of immortality!

Thus stood he in the morning light,
Looking upon that Mountain's height,
When over his young cheeks there came
The lightnings of immortal fame.
Unsandaling, now, his feet of snow,
He rose up from the Vale below—
(Climbing Virginia's rocky wall—)
And wrote his name above them all!
Then, shouting with exultant voice,
Which made the very Stars rejoice,
Cried to the Angel in the Sun,
And to the name of Washington,
With transports that made glad the sky
With voice of immortality—
    Gloria in Excelsis Domino!

An Eagle, that had built her nest
High on the rocky Mountain's crest,

Seeing him there at such a height,
Exulting in the morning light,
Rose with exultant scream on high,
And, climbing to the noonday sky,
Cried to the Angel in the Sun,
And to the Name of Washington—
This is the boy that cannot die—
The Child of Immortality!

Thus stood he on that Mountain brow,
Exulting in the Morning's glow—
The fairest of that heavenly Band
Of young Immortals, from the Land
Of Love—a Pilgrim of the Sun—
Shouting the name of Washington—
With hand onstretched above to bless
The world below with happiness—
Wearing upon his brow of day
The Chaplet of immortal bay,
Fed by the Eagles of the sky
With food of immortality;
For, like the Eaglets in their nest,
Was he by their affection blest.
There, Cupid, with the milk-white Doves
Of Venus, from the Paphian Groves,
Came flocking, with exultant joy,
To give delight to that young boy—
While Angels from the far-off skies
Rivers of rapturous melodies
Poured on his soul, till he became
The richest of the Heirs of Fame.

Thus stood he on that Mountain brow,
Exulting in the Morning's glow;
When he beheld, at early morn,
From the bright land where he was born,

A Maiden fairer than the Moon,
And brighter than the Sun at noon,
Coming along the Vale below,
With rosy Chaplets on her brow.
Hearing the Eagles scream his name,
She suddenly stopped with cheeks of flame,
And, lifting up her deep blue eyes
Flashing the glory of the skies,
(Seeing him there at such a height,
Exulting in the Morning light—)
Cried to the Angel in the Sun,
And to the name of Washington—
> *Victoria Aleluatica!*

Thus stood he on that Mountain's brow,
The Sun that made the Moon below—
Hearing the Eagles scream his name—
The richest of the Heirs of Fame—
When, on the pinions of the Dove,
She visited his Home of Love,
With Sonnets of the fairest flowers
That ever blew in bosky bowers—
The odor of whose soul did plain
To him her heart's melodious pain.
Seeing from his high Mountain's brow,
This Angel in the Vale below,
Looking up at him with her eyes
Flashing the glory of the skies—
He felt, with an impatient heat,
His heart within his bosom beat.
But as she was not made to climb
To that great Mountain's height sublime,
To wed her, he was doomed to go
Down in the verdant Vale below—
For nothing now could give him rest,
But that sweet Joy that made him blest;

For Beauty, with her love divine,
Intoxicates the soul like wine.
Thus, glory-crowned, in robes of light,
He soared up from the World's dark night,
And sitting on the highest Sills,
With Angels, on the Eternal Hills,
Hears Heaven's immortal music roll
Down God's great Ages through his soul.
                    Te Deum Laudamus!

———◆———

THE BEAUTIFUL SILENCE:

Composed on seeing a beautiful Deaf-Mute Lady.

Thou art the Angel of the voiceful silence
    Christ left behind him when he went to God—
Fair to the Earth as to the Sea those Islands
    Where Beauty with the Graces took up their abode;
For, as Cytheria to the ever-sounding Sea
Was silent, when most beautiful, art thou to all things
        unto me.

Thy knowledge comes to thee down-flowing,
    As does an Angel's, free from earthly sin,
Out of the life divine of God all-knowing—
    Ours from without—thine to thy soul within—
And, Angel-like, although thy lips are mute,
Like Israfel in Heaven, thy heartstrings are a lute.

All those discordant, ever-jarring noises
    Which grate upon our souls, thou hast not heard;
But thou dost hear, unheard to us, the heavenly Voices
    Made audible to thee through God's most holy Word;
For, being an Angel, thou dost use an Angel's tongue,
Silence, God's holy language, sweeter far than Song.

Like some sweet Star afar off in the ether,
   Singing, while shining, in the Heavens above,
For all the rest to hear, but hearing neither—
   Yet still dispensing rarest gifts of love—
So, thy dear soul sits here in peace secure,
Shrined in the milk-white Temple of thy body pure.

Thou dost inherit all that heavenly treasure—
   Direct communion with the Life Divine—
Which Angel's language, Silence without measure,
   Can only give to such sweet souls as thine ;
For, through thine isolation, thou dost live
The life divine that only Death to other souls can give.

God could bestow on me no heavenlier Vision
   Than gazing on thy form, dear heavenly One !
Thinking of thee, I rove through Fields Elysian,
   In mental walks, with His dear blessed Son !
For, where thou art, there Christ must ever be ;
And there, or not, thy presence makes him there to me.

Thou art more beautiful than milk-white Una—
   Meeker than Mercy, gentler than sweet Sleep—
Fairer to me than to Endymion Luna—
   Coming from Heaven to teach me how to weep,
With piteous love, for thy dear, blessed sake—
Whose lamb-like innocence should make the World's heart
   break.

A living music, voiceless, yet forever
   Speaking such words as tongue can never tell ;
A heavenly Hymn, whose echoes shall die never,
   As long as this sweet Song shall say *Farewell ;*
For, fare-thee-well comes freer from the heart
Of those who meet, than those who say it when they part.

Two of the golden strings of thy dear harp are broken,
   Leaving the harp-strings of thy spirit still complete ;
Words, by thy tongue, have never yet been spoken,
   Yet, thy dear soul doth warble words most sweet,
Whereon blest Spirits, from their bright Abode,
Make music such as please the very Ears of God,

Thou hearest the far-off, endless chiming
   Of the eternal music of the Spheres ;
And knowest, by intuition, all the rhyming
   Of all the Cycles of the rhythmic years ;
And walkest, in spirit, where no foot has ever trod,
With beautiful, milk-white feet up to the shining Mount
   of God.

Oh ! God ! if this dear, heavenly creature
   Were only mine, what would I do for thee ?
Seeing her wearing here each God-like feature
   Of Christ, while Incarnating Heaven for me ;
And living here on earth the life divine,
And, Star-like, singing, shining while she makes me shine.

TONTINE HOTEL, NEW HAVEN, October 31, 1851.

———◆———

THE CRUCIFIXION.

From the Temple torn asunder
   Of his God-Humanity,
Lofty piles of echoing thunder
   Rolled in groans of agony !

From his heart, the blood down-spilling,
   Incense-smoke of pain was sent,
Blotting out the Sun, while filling
   Heaven and Earth with wonderment !

VILLA ALLEGRA, GA., August 8, 1836.

3

THE BELLES OF TONTINE.

A LYRIC IN PRAISE OF FAIR LADIES.

In this city, in the Palace,
Called the Tontine, kept by Allis,
Standing Eastward of the Eden of the Green—
Dwells the Lady Ellen-Mary,
Who is of her charms so chary,
That opinions never vary
Of her beauty in Tontine—
All agreeing she is BELLE of this Tontine—
Cynosure of all the lesser lights that twinkle in Tontine.

But, within this stately Palace,
Called the Tontine, kept by Allis,
Standing Eastward of the Eden of the Green—
Dwells another Lady Mary,
Of whose charms opinions vary—
Lovers talking quite contrary
Of her beauty in Tontine;
All agreeing she will " *do* " for this Tontine—
But that Lady Ellen-Mary is the BELLE of this Tontine.

Thus, within this stately Palace,
Called the Tontine, kept by Allis,
Standing Eastward of the Eden of the Green—
Dwell the two fair Virgin Maries,
Beautiful as two contraries
Can be, who are rival Fairies
Of each other in Tontine—
All agreeing each will " *do* " for this Tontine—
But that Lady Ellen-Mary is the BELLE of this Tontine.

So, within this stately Palace,
Called the Tontine, kept by Allis,
Standing Eastward of the Eden of the Green—

Dwells the one with eyes of azure,
Melting in her soul of pleasure,
Shedding love-light, without measure,
On her lovers in Tontine—
All agreeing she is BELLE of this Tontine—
Cynosure of all the lesser lights that twinkle in Tontine.

But, within this stately Palace,
Called the Tontine, kept by Allis,
Standing Eastward of the Eden of the Green—
Shine the other's eyes, all darkling,
With the love-light in them sparkling,
Darker brows above them circling,
Making Heaven of this Tontine ;
Though they say that she will " *do* " for this Tontine—
And that Lady Ellen-Mary is the BELLE of this Tontine.

Thus, within this stately Palace,
Called the Tontine, kept by Allis,
Standing Eastward of the Eden of the Green—
Dwell the two renowned in story,
And, that neither may be sorry,
I will crown them both with glory,
As the BELLES of this Tontine—
Notwithstanding what was said, in this Tontine,
Of the Lady Ellen-Mary being BELLE of this Tontine.

Now, within this stately Palace,
Called the Tontine, kept by Allis,
Standing Eastward of the Eden of the Green—
These two golden BELLES are ringing
In the Song that I am singing,
Which its way to Heaven goes winging
With these BEAUTIES of Tontine —
Fiery chariot rising Heavenward from Tontine—
Bearing up these BELLES to glory from the Chebar of Tontine.

TONTINE HOTEL, NEW HAVEN, August 10th, 1851.

APOLLO.

What are stars, but hieroglyphics of God's glory writ in
　　lightning
　　On the wide-unfolded pages of the azure scroll above?
But the quenchless apotheoses of thoughts forever brightening
　　In the mighty Mind immortal of the God, whose name is
　　Love?
Diamond letters sculptured, rising, on the azure ether pages,
　　That now sing to one another—unto one another shine—
God's eternal Scripture talking, through the midnight, to the
　　Ages,
　　Of the life that is immortal, of the life that is divine—
　　Life that *cannot* be immortal, but the life that is divine.

Like some deep, impetuous river from the fountains everlasting,
　　Down the serpentine soft valley of the vistas of all Time,
Over cataracts of adamant uplifted into mountains,
　　Soared his soul to God in thunder on the wings of thought
　　sublime,
With the rising golden glory of the sun in ministrations,
　　Making oceans metropolitan of splendor for the dawn—
Piling pyramid on pyramid of music for the nations—
　　Sings the Angel who sits shining everlasting in the sun,
　　For the stars, which are the echoes of the shining of the sun.

Like the lightnings piled on lightnings, ever rising, never
　　reaching,
　　In one monument of glory towards the golden gates of God—
Voicing out themselves in thunder upon thunder in their
　　preaching,
　　Piled this Cyclop up his Epic where the Angels never trod.
Like the fountains everlasting that forever more are flowing
　　From the throne within the centre of the City built on high,
With their genial irrigation life forever more bestowing—
　　Flows his lucid, liquid river through the gardens of the sky,
　　For the stars forever blooming in the gardens of the sky.

LILY ADAIR.

On the beryl-rimmed rebecs of Ruby,
  Brought fresh from the hyaline streams,
She played, on the banks of the Yuba,
  Such songs as she heard in her dreams.
Like the heavens, when the stars from their eyries
  Look down through the ebon night air,
Were the groves by the Ouphantic Fairies
  Lit up for my Lily Adair—
  For my child-like Lily Adair—
  For my heaven-born Lily Adair—
For my beautiful, dutiful Lily Adair.

Like two rose-leaves in sunshine when blowing,
  Just curled softly, gently apart,
Were her lips by her passion, while growing
  In perfume on the stalk of her heart.
As mild as the sweet influences
  Of the Pleiades 'pregning the air—
More mild than the throned Excellencies
  Up in heaven, was my Lily Adair—
  Was my Christ-like Lily Adair—
  Was my lamb-like Lily Adair—
Was my beautiful, dutiful Lily Adair.

At the birth of this fair virgin Vestal,
  She was taken for Venus' child ;
And her voice, though like diamond in crystal,
  Was not more melodious than mild.
Like the moon in her soft silver splendor,
  She was shrined in her own, past compare,
For no Angel in heaven was more tender
  Than my beautiful Lily Adair—
  Than my dove-like Lily Adair—
  Than my saint-like Lily Adair—
Than my beautiful, dutiful Lily Adair.

3*

Thus she stood on the arabesque borders
　　Of the beautiful blossoms that blew
On the banks of the crystalline waters,
　　Every morn, in the diaphane dew.
The flowers, they were radiant with glory,
　　And shed such perfume on the air,
That my soul, now to want them, feels sorry,
　　And bleeds for my Lily Adair—
　　For my much-loved Lily Adair—
　　For my long-lost Lily Adair—
For my beautiful, dutiful Lily Adair.

———✦———

VALETE OMNIA.

Into that Morning Land of Beauty,
My Pattern Christ—Christ that doth truly know
All my desire has been to do my duty—
Out of this Evening Land of Grief I go—
　　I go where the wild Roses blow
On the banks of that Beautiful River whose flow
　　　Is under the grave below—
　　　All under the grave below!
　Oh! give me that crystal Nepenthe,
　Where the Waters of Life freely flow;
　I will drink to my bright Euryanthe
　In the Place where the wild Roses blow—
　The Place where I long now to go—
On the banks of that Beautiful River whose flow
　　　Is under the grave below—
　　　All under the grave below!
　　Then, farewell, father! farewell, mother!
　　Farewell, sister! farewell, brother!
　　I go where the wild Roses blow
　　　All under the grave below!

"But will you return to us never?"
    Said they, "On some future day,
    In the Month of May,
From the Place where the wild Roses blow!"
    And I answered them, No, no, no!
        Oh! no, no, no!
        No, never—never—never!

I long for that endless existence,
Where the Morning is just like the Even;
Where the Angels receive their subsistence
From the undefiled Fountains of Heaven—
    In the Place where the wild Roses grow
On the banks of that Beautiful River whose flow
    Is under the grave below—
    All under the grave below!
The great golden hand on the Adamant Dial
Of the Clock of Eternity pauses in Heaven!
From Death's bony hand I now empty the Phial—
And the Morning is just like the Even!
    I go where the wild Roses blow
On the banks of that Beautiful River whose flow
    Is under the grave below!
    All under the grave below!
    Then, farewell, father! farewell, mother!
    Farewell, sister! farewell, brother!
    I go where the wild Roses blow
    All under the grave below!
"Now he will return to us never,"
    Said they, "On some future day,
    In the Month of May,
From the Place where the wild Roses blow!"
    And I answered them, No, no, no!
        Oh! no, no, no!
        No—NEVER—NEVER—NEVER!

TO THE QUEEN OF MY HEART.

"I have drunk Lethe ?"—JOHN WEBSTER, 1665.

I will give you Bread of Angels, sweeter far than any honey—
   Whiter far, in its clear sweetness, than the snow of Leda's
     love—
In the South-Land, far away, beneath the skies forever sunny,
   It was dropt upon the golden flowers in dew-drops from
     above.
Then no heart can speak so sweetly as the heart that has been
   broken,
   As the Swan will sing the sweetest on the day that it must die ;
And no word can ever charm us like the words that we hear
   spoken
   By our friend upon his deathbed, when he knows that Heaven
     is nigh.

Pure as drops of dew congealed to Pearls beneath the troubled
   Ocean,
   That the Divers value most because found deepest in the Sea ;
Are the words that now well up from out my heart's divine
   devotion,
   And here sparkle in this JEWEL set to shrine my love for thee.
Like the Mirror in the Minor * of the City of the Sages,
   Which betrayed the Grecian enemy afar off on the sea ;
But, when broken, left them prostrate to their wantonness for
   Ages,—
   So my heart will bow to Sorrow if once broken, love! by thee !

If thou art the only Pharos that can light my soul, at even,
   When my Bark of Life is wrecking on Time's Ocean tempest-
    tost,
By what Beacon shall my spirit reach the peaceful Port of
   Heaven,
   From the Valley of Dark Shadows where so many men are lost?

* Light House, or Pharos.

Many Palm trees are at Elim—many brooks of running water—
  For the feeding of the hungry—for the quenching of their
    thirst—
But the Fountain opened freely on Mount Zion for her Daughter
  Is the sweetest ever tasted—for this latest one was first.

Hear you not the cooing Turtles in the Willows giving warning
  That the Golden Time for singing on the earth will soon
    arrive?
When the Morning shall be Evening, for the Evening shall be
  Morning—
  And the soul, possessing Heaven, no more for Heaven on
    earth shall strive.
Like the Rose that gives out odor only when we come to
  trample
  On its petals, from my bruised heart flows the incense of my
    song—
Like the golden clouds of fragrance from the Altar in the
  Temple—
  For the soul will show the sweetest under deepest sense of
    wrong.

I am mourning for the downfall of my Daughter of sweet Zion!
  For she would not hear my counsel—ah! her heart within
    was dead!
Like the Holy City Salem treated Judah's Lamb-like Lion,
  Till the Crown, that God had crowned her with, was taken
    from her head!
I will give you Bread of Angels, sweeter far than any honey—
  Whiter far, in its clear sweetness, than the snow of Leda's
    love—
In the South-Land, far away, beneath the skies forever sunny,
  It was dropt upon the golden flowers in dew-drops from above.

THE FALL OF USHER.

" Thou wert the Morning Star among the living,
Ere thy fair light had fled ;
But, having died, thou art like Hesperus giving
New splendor to the dead."—PLATO'S ASTER.

" Thou art gone to the grave ! " but thy spirit is shining,
  And singing afar in the REALMS OF THE BLEST ;
While the living are left by thy cold grave reclining,
  And mourning for thee while they long for thy rest—
  Left mourning for thee while they long for thy rest !

" Thou art gone to the grave ! " thou art gone where thy
      slumber
  No more shall be broken by sorrow or pain—
Soon to rise with that host which no mortal can number,
  To lie down no more in that Valley again !
  No more to lie down in that Valley again !

" Thou art gone to the grave ! " there is none can restore thee,
  Or bring thee again from that SILENT ABODE !
But the CONQUEROR OF DEATH went to dwell there before thee,
  And HE has prepared thee the way to thy God !
  Prepared thee the way to thy BEAUTIFUL GOD !

" Thou art gone to the grave ! " thou art silently sleeping
  A sleep which no sorrow shall ever molest ;
And, in longing for which, my poor heart now is keeping
  This silent lament in its grave in my breast !
  Like Shelley for Keats, in its grave in my breast !

" Thou art gone to the grave ! " let the dark Weeping Willow
  Bend over thy grave where thy beauty was laid !
While thy form, thus reclined on the earth for its pillow,
  Shall live in the Spring-flowers which bloom at thy head—
  To feed the young Butterflies born at thy head.

"Thou art gone to the grave!" where the Violets are springing,
    And feeding upon thee above the damp sod,
Now thy Pandemos mourns, while thy spirit is singing,
    And drinking delight from the FOUNTAINS OF GOD—
With thine ULLALUME lost from the FOUNTAINS OF GOD.

VILLA ALLEGRA, GA.

——❖——

ROSALIE LEE.

"Les Anges ne sont plus pures que le cœur d' un jeune homme qui aime en verite."—MADAME DUDEVANT.

On the banks of the yellow lilies,
    Where the cool wave wanders by,
All bedamasked with Daffodillies,
    And the bee-beset Crowtie;
More mild than the Paphian Luna
    To her nude Nymphs on the Sea,
There dwelt, with her milk-white Una,
        My beautiful Rosalie Lee—
        My high-born Rosalie Lee—
        My child-like Rosalie Lee—
My beautiful, dutiful Rosalie Lee.

More coy than the wild Goldfinches,
    When they hunt for the Butterfly,
Which the dew of the morning quenches,
    In the psychical month July;
Like an opaline Dove's neck chiming
    Cherubic beauty for me,
Were her ovaline arms in their rhyming,
        Of my beautiful Rosalie Lee—
        Of my lamb-like Rosalie Lee—
        Of my Heaven-born Rosalie Lee—
Of my beautiful, dutiful Rosalie Lee.

Many mellow Cydonian Suckets,
    Sweet apples, anthosmial, divine,
From the Ruby-rimmed Beryline buckets,
    Star-gemmed, lily-shaped, hyaline—
Like that sweet golden goblet found growing
    On the wild emerald Cucumber-tree—
Rich, brilliant, like Chrysopraz blowing—
        I then brought to my Rosalie Lee—
        To my lamb-like Rosalie Lee—
        To my Dove-like Rosalie Lee—
    To my beautiful, dutiful Rosalie Lee.

Warbling her wood-notes wild, she wended
    Her way with the turtle Doves,
And the Wood-nymphs weird that attended
    Her steps through the flowery groves.
In the light of her eyes of azure,
    My soul seemed on earth to see
All that Heaven could give me of pleasure,
        With my beautiful Rosalie Lee—
        With my Heaven-born Rosalie Lee—
        With my Christ-like Rosalie Lee—
    With my beautiful, dutiful Rosalie Lee.

But my darling Ulpsyche sighing
    Her soul out to give me delight,
Went away with the great Undying
    To the Courts of the Heavenly Light.
Through an arc made in the azure
    Of God's azimuth, Heaven to see,
There to dwell with the Angels in pleasure—
        Went my beautiful Rosalie Lee—
        Went my fair-browed Rosalie Lee—
        Went my much loved Rosalie Lee—
    Went my beautiful, dutiful Rosalie Lee.

Through the Valley of Avalon lonely,
   By the light of the argentine Moon,
From the presence that lived for her only
   On the banks of the Rivers of Rune;
Through the Star-Islands studding the Ether,
   With the Angels that took her from me—
(Though my soul in its sorrow went with her—)
   Soared my beautiful Rosalie Lee—
   Soared my Christ-like Rosalie Lee—
   Soared my God-loved Rosalie Lee—
Soared my beautiful, dutiful Rosalie Lee.

———✧———

ROSIGNOL SUEDOIS.

"Lord! what music hast thou prepared for the Saints in Heaven, if such music as this is to be heard by bad men upon the earth?"—IZAAK WALTON.

Thy voice, oh! Vesper of the starry even!
   Rained round my soul such golden songs last night,
It seemed some fiery star had burst in Heaven,
   And scattered on the earth its crown of light;
Which so inspired me, that I felt like weeping,
   But could not weep, my joy was so divine,—
Such harvests of rich bliss forever reaping,
   I seemed in Heaven—for Heaven was surely thine.

Such sweet, melodious plaints were round me raining,
   Filling my soul with undefiled delight—
Like Joy's sweet voice of too much bliss complaining—
   It seemed that Heaven was opened to my sight;
And I could hear the blissful Angels singing,
   And see the heavenly hosts around me fly;
And felt such instinct in my soul for flying,
   That I, too, seemed an Angel, never born to die.

As if the Lord the bended Heavens had cloven,
 And down descending from his throne on high,
With fiery vestments out of lightnings woven,
 Had clothed my soul for immortality.
For I could hear the gates of glory moving
 On musical, golden hinges, far above,
And see God's smile the works of Christ approving,
 Because Christ's works are moulded in His love.

Oh ! such another night of heavenly rapture,
 Would shrive my soul of every earthly sin,
For thy sweet songs inspire me more than Scripture—
 Thou Angel at Heaven's gates to let me in !
For they have purged me of all dross of sorrow,
 And purified me for the life to be,
And fitted me to go to Heaven to-morrow,
 And I would go—if I could only go with thee.

BIRTH OF THE NEW LOVE.

AN ALMAN FOR THE LUTE.

O ! the day that we went sailing,
 A-sailing on the sea—
Then it was that, Love prevailing,
 I first gave my soul to thee.
Far more restless than the ocean,
 As our boat plowed through the brine,
Was my heart, in its emotion,
 As my breast heaved close to thine.
O ! the day that we went sailing
 Upon that summer sea ;

Then it was that, Love prevailing,
  I first gave my soul to thee—
  Gave my soul alone to thee!
  Gave my heart and soul to thee!

Then thy dark eyes, mildly tender,
  Beamed responsive unto mine,
As my soul, in words of splendor,
  Soared to glory over thine.
When you talked, it was like singing;
  When you sang, it was to me
Far above an Angel's, bringing
  Down the Heavens upon the sea!
O! the day that we went sailing,
  A-sailing on the sea;
Then it was that, Love prevailing,
  I first gave my soul to thee—
  Gave my soul alone to thee!
  Gave my heart and soul to thee!

Then I asked you, in my blindness,
  To give light unto mine eyes;
And you answered, in your kindness,
  With a vision from the skies!
Answered not alone with blushes,
  But with trembling lips to mine,
As the blood of life now rushes
  Through my soul to mix with thine!
O! the day that we went sailing
  Upon that summer sea;
Then it was that, Love prevailing,
  I first gave my soul to thee—
  Gave my soul alone to thee!
  Gave my heart and soul to thee!

AMORE DIVINO.

My rapturous soul, entranced, now naked lies
   Humbled before thee in the very dust—
Crying unto thee, as some Christian cries
   Unto the God in whom he puts his trust.

Like the great golden Stairs that towered sublime,
   Which Jacob saw on Bethel plain at even ;
Thou art the Ladder by which I now climb
   From this dark world up to my Home in Heaven.

When thy sweet beauty first to me was given,
   My soul, by gazing on thee, grew like thine ;
For thou hadst power to change this world to Heaven,
   And make all things, like thy dear self, divine.

I would, but to secure this heavenly Crown,
   Go from the Garden of Gethsemane,
And there on Calvary lay my body down,
   If, being crucified, my soul could dwell with thee.

Scourgings would be to this fond heart of mine,
   The soft caressings of impassioned pain ;
Wormwood, Ambrosia—death, the life divine—
   If I, in Kingdom Come, with thee could reign.

I would be nailed upon the Cross to die,
   To drink the healing Wellsprings of thy love ;
For I should see, in my great agony,
   The Gates of Glory opening there above.

For being laid into the grave would be
   A prelude to that resurrection bliss—
That Crown of Glory I should wear with thee
   In Heaven above of future happiness.

Where my entranced soul should ever hear
    The jubilant shout of the Angelic Choir,
And all the Morning Stars, from year to year,
    Answering the Sons of God with lips of fire.

TONTINE HOTEL, NEW HAVEN, CONN., July 4, 1851.

----◆----

THE MOON OF MOBILE.

The Song that she sang was all written
    In rubies that sparkled like wine,
Like the Morning Star burning, new litten
    By the tablets of diamond divine.
Like some ravishing sound made from divers
    Sweet instruments fluting in June,
From her soul flowed those musical rivers
    Of Odin, called the rivers of Rune.
Then come to my bower, sweet Angel!
    Love's Fountain of Life to unseal; *
You shall live in this amber Evangel,
    Sweet Ellen! the Pride of Mobile!
Sweet Ellen! dear Ellen! the Maid of Mobile!
My Mary, mavourneen, the Moon of Mobile!

On the rhythmical rounds of the rhyming
    Of this Lyrical Ladder she rode,
Like an Angel that sings in his climbing
    To the Gates of the City of God.
Like the Gods when they feed on the blisses
    Of the undefiled glories above;
So my soul drank delight from the kisses
    Of the lips of my beautiful love.
Then come to my bower, sweet Angel!
    Love's fountain of life to unseal;

* "A garden enclosed is my sister, my spouse; a spring shut up, a fountain sealed."—SOLOMON'S SONGS, IV, 12.

You shall live in this amber Evangel,
  Sweet Ellen! the Pride of Mobile!
Sweet Ellen! dear Ellen! the Maid of Mobile!
My Mary, mavourneen, the Moon of Mobile!

Her soul sparkled bright through the azure
  Of her violet eyes full of light,
Like young Venus, long absent from pleasure,
  When Adonis first comes in her sight.
As the Angels clomb up, late at even,
  From the Bethel of Jacob above;
So, the Angels of thought go to Heaven
  On the rounds of the Ladder of Love.
Then come to my bower, sweet Angel!
  Love's Fountain of Life to unseal;
You shall live in this amber Evangel,
  Sweet Ellen the Pride of Mobile!
Sweet Ellen! dear Ellen! the Maid of Mobile!
My Mary, mavourneen, the Moon of Mobile!

Prester John never sent, out of duty,
  From the City of Heaven, called Cansay,*
Any maiden so rich in all beauty,
  To the Lord of the Isles of Cathay.†
Like the Moon in her soft silver azure,
  Star-engirdled, sweet Queen of the Night!
So she stood in this Palace of Pleasure,
  Circled round by the Swans of Delight.
Then come to my bower, sweet Angel!
  Love's Fountain of Life to unseal;
You shall live in this amber Evangel,
  Sweet Ellen! the Pride of Mobile!
Sweet Ellen! dear Ellen! the Maid of Mobile!
  My Mary, mavourneen, the Moon of Mobile!

TONTINE HOTEL, NEW HAVEN, CONN., August 20, 1851.

---

* Cansay, or Kin-sai, which signifies the City of Heaven. It was the capital of Southern China, under the dynasty of the Song.

† Ghenhis Khan, whose palace was built of pure gold, and ornamented with the finest of Jewels.

ELEGY OF TEARS.

WRITTEN ON HEARING OF THE DEATH OF MY SISTER.

Like the pious pathetical Rachel in Ramah,
  Who mourned for her beautiful band!
Oh! pour out your souls to the merciful Tamer
  Of the Lions in the Lion-Land!
As she would not be comforted, crying forever,
  In life, after death, for the loved, early lost!
Oh! weep for your mother! but smile never, never—
  For what have your souls, since her death, now to boast?
    Then weep, orphan children! weep! weep!

Oh! weep out your hearts for the loss of your mother!
  Pour, pour out your souls in one pitiful rain!
For ye never can know, in this wide world, another
  So true to your hearts as that mother has been!
Wail aloud, oh! ye orphans! like Zion's sweet daughters,
  When they poured out their hearts in such heartmelting tears,
By the willows that wept over Babylon's waters,
  That their grief took for pay all eternity's years!
    Then weep, orphan children! weep! weep!

Like the pitiful wail of that BEAUTIFUL LION
  Of Judah, in the forests of Lebanon lone,
When he mourned for the loss of the daughter of Zion,
  Who killed all the Prophets of God, one by one;
Let your dark ebon locks, like the limbs of the willow,
  Rain down from your brows on her dark narrow bed,
In one stream of despair, as ye kneel by the pillow
  Of earth, tear-baptized, newly heaped on the dead!
    Then weep, orphan children! weep! weep!
Weep, weep for your mother! weep! weep!

NEW HAVEN, CONN., May 20, 1851.

THE LADY ALICE.

The night is serene with pleasure—
    Balmy the air—
For the Moon makes the icy azure
    Argently clear;
While the Stars with their music make measure
    To mine down here—
    My song down here—
    My beautiful song down here.

Pale light from her orb is raining
    On earth—the sea;
While I am on earth complaining
    Of one to me
More fair than the Moon now waning—
    More pure than she—
    More fair than she—
    More womanly pure than she.

She lives in her golden palace
    Beside the sea;
And her name is the Lady Alice—
    So dear to me!
And she drinks from her crystal Chalice
    Sweet wine so free—
    White wine so free—
    Because her pure heart is free.

She sings, while the Angels listen
    With pure delight!
And the Stars with new glory glisten,
    And laughter bright;
While my heart, in its narrow prison,
    Doth pine to-night—
    Pine all the night—
    For want of my Moon to-night.

She smiles, while my soul is sorry
    With love divine;
And the Stars hear in Heaven the story
    Which makes me pine!
I would give all their crowns of glory
    If she were mine—
      Were only mine—
    Were only forever mine.

Oh! come from thy golden Palace,
    Sweet Lady bright!
And fill up this empty Chalice
    With wine to-night!—
I drink to my Lady Alice!
    My soul's delight—
    Heart—soul's delight—
    My ever divine delight!

————❖————

CELUTA.

"MAID OF MY LOVE"

Seraph-faced was my Celuta,
Meekly mild her Angel-beauty—
Doing good she deemed her duty—
    Loving all she wished to know;
All God's highest, holiest nature
Was expressed in this sweet creature—
Heaven's own face lived in each feature,
    In the days of long ago.

On the Asphodelian Meadows,
In the cool refreshing shadows
Of the Trees of God, we made us
    Beds of flowers as white as snow,

Where we lay, while on before us
Flew the Angel-Hours in chorus,
Making all the air odorous,
    In the days of long ago.

Like some Cygnet, silver-breasted,
In the rushes newly nested ;
Or, like Moses when he rested,
    Cradled on the wave below;
So my head lay on the pillow
Of her bosom's milky billow,
Underneath the Weeping Willow,
    In the days of long ago.

There, with watchful eyes, beholding
God's sweet Eden-flower unfolding
All her radiant beauty, holding
    To the Cross of Christ below;
I did seem in God's own presence,
In the realms of peaceful pleasance,
Like our First-born Eden-peasants
    In the days of long ago.

As the glorified Orion,
From the Mount that he did die on,
Saw the Pleiades of Zion,
    Clad in garments white as snow,
Up in Heaven in glory pining,
Through my tears, (deep grief divining,)
I now see the far-off shining
    Of the days of long ago.

Grief, not age, has made me hoary !
Death has left my whole soul sorry !
This, my blue-eyed MORNING GLORY !
    Thou dost more than truly know !

But the hopes that we now cherish
In our souls, shall never perish,
Till an Eden there shall flourish,
    As in the days of long ago.

How my soul doth long to meet thee !
With what rapture could I greet thee !
Yielding, lest I should entreat thee,
    With my heart's deep overflow,
In the flower-embalmed abysses
Of the Eden-wildernesses,
Filled with Heaven's immortal blisses,
    As in days of long ago.

THE BRIGHT NEW MOON OF LOVE.

At the dawn she stood debating
    With the angels at the door
Of Christ's sepulchre, in waiting
    For his body evermore.
Pure as white-robed Faith to Sorrow,
    Pointing back to Heaven above—
(Happy Day for every morrow)—
    Was the Bright New Moon of Love.

Nun-like, chaste in her devotion,
    All the stars in heaven on high,
With their radiant, rhythmic motion,
    Chimed in with her from the sky.
Sweeter far than day when breaking,
    Angel-like, in heaven above,
On the traveler lost, when waking,
    Was the Bright New Moon of Love.

Thus she glorified all sweetness
  With the angel-light she shed
From her soul in such completeness,
  That she beautified the dead.
When an Angel, sent on duty
  From his Father's throne above,
Saw the heaven-surpassing beauty
  Of this Bright New Moon of Love.

For the Truth she loved was Beauty,
  Because Beauty was her Truth;
And to love her was his duty,
  Such as Boaz owed to Ruth.
God had set his seal upon her,
  Her divinity to prove,
And this Angel wooed her—won her—
  Won the Bright New Moon of Love.

Thus the Mission of True Woman
  She did act out in this life—
Showed the Divine in the Human,
  In her duties of the Wife.
For the Heaven that he had taken,
  Was so much like that above,
That the Heaven he had forsaken,
  Was the Bright New Moon of Love.

For the kingdom of Christ's glory,
  Angel-chanted at her birth,
Is the theme now of the story
  Which I warble through the earth.
And because this fallen Angel
  Took her home to heaven above,
I now write this NEW EVANGEL
  Of the Bright New Moon of Love.

MORCIA FUNEBRE;

OR,

A REQUIEM ON THE DEATH OF HENRY CLAY.

Toll, toll, toll !
Let your great Thor-hammer strike upon the bell,
Crushing from out his iron heart the dole—
To sable all the world with his funeral knell !
For the passing into glory of his soul—
For the Requiem of the soaring into glory of his soul !
Then toll, toll, toll !
Till the billows of your moan,
From your iron heart that inwardly doth groan, groan, groan,
Shall, like raging seas, roll on, on, on,
To the Goal, to the Goal—
To the glorious golden Goal—
Where that mighty Man is gone—
To the Kingdom of the Soul—
From this Valley of Dark Shadows to the Kingdom of the
Soul !
Toll, toll, toll !
Till the Angels lean down from their blest Abode,
To hear the thunders of your Requiem roll, roll, roll—
Foaming against the white shore of the feet of God !
For the passing into glory of his soul—
For the Requiem of the soaring into glory of his soul !
Then toll, toll, toll !
Till the billows of your moan,
From your iron heart that inwardly doth groan, groan, groan,
Shall, like raging seas, roll on, on, on,
To the Goal, to the Goal—
To the glorious golden Goal—
Where that mighty Man is gone—
To the Kingdom of the Soul—
From this Valley of Dark Shadows to the Kingdom of the
Soul !

Toll, toll, toll !
Like the billows of some whirlwind-tortured sea,
  Let the pathetic thunders of your ringing roll, roll, roll—
Rising, till they shall all arrive as far as unto thee !
    For the passing into glory of his soul—
For the Requiem of the soaring into glory of his soul !
      Then toll, toll, toll !
    Till the billows of your moan,
From your iron heart that inwardly doth groan, groan, groan,
      Shall, like raging seas, roll on, on, on,
        To the Goal, to the Goal—
        To the glorious golden Goal—
      Where that mighty Man is gone—
        To the Kingdom of the Soul—
From this Valley of Dark Shadows to the Kingdom of the
    Soul !

TONTINE HOTEL, NEW HAVEN, CONN., JULY 5, 1852.

————❖————

THE RISING OF THE NATIONS.

Millions of millions now are groaning, groaning
  Beneath the grinding weight of Despotism,
While bloody Anarchy, unmindful of their moaning,
  Plunges them deeper into Hell's unsunned Abyssum !
While Earth, now slimed beneath his vile pollution,
  Echoes the wailings of their desolation,
Until the remnant, ripe for revolution,
  Answers the music of their soul's salvation,
Uttered by Liberty upon th' immortal Mountains,
  From all the vallies, out of every habitation—
Coming, like many rills from new-born Fountains
  Fresh opened in the Earth from long-descending rains,

Which, gathering into one great onward rushing river,
    Distending, overflows its banks, till all the plains
Are inundated with its everspreading waters—
    Still gathering volume as it flows forever ;—
So did they gather in one mighty multitude,
    As if the Nations from the four great quarters
Of all the earth had migrated in one great flood,
    With one great common sympathy, to overthrow
    This mighty Monarch of the world—this foe
To human greatness—this great Devil to the Free—
This damned Abaddon of the Sons of Anarchy !

Now louder than the loud tumultuous Ocean
    Stormed into passion by the ever-roaring Winds—
Come the loud shouts from all those multitudes in motion,
    Chorusing the lightnings of these million mighty minds—
Answering the Bugle-blasts from out the Mountains,
    Blown from the lips of ever-living Liberty—
Louder than thunders of ten thousand fountains
    Leaping down cataracts of Adamant exultingly—
Impatient to become the Children of the Sea !
    So did these living Columns of the indignant Free,
Sweep onward to the Angel-voice of Liberty,
    Over the desperate cataracts of Anarchy,
Down to the opening Ocean of their Destiny—
    Piling their rafts of slain along the vallies,
Like fallen forests—prostrate Monuments of slaughter—
    To fatten Earth, or fill up Buzzard's billies—
For future Tyrants, now, shall know no quarter !

Millions now wait, with breathless expectation,
    To hail the Advent of the Lord's annointed—
The First-born Child of God, whose coronation
    Now begins, from old upon this blessed day appointed.

So, now, the Hallelujahs of the immortal Free
Proclaim him King whose name is LIBERTY !

Now, with the thunder-shout of eloquent persuasion,
    From all the myriads here assembled to give praise,
Answering the booming cannons on the occasion—
    Battering the Gates of Heaven with repercussive blaze—
They spread the News, from Nation unto Nation,
    With unrestrained delight, that they are free !
Till all the Mountains echo back their jubilation,
    Teaching the Earth the glorious name of Liberty !
Hosanna in Excelsis, was the joyful thunder
    That rose up from their souls from morn till even,
Dying, at midnight, into silence deep as wonder,
As dies some Christian knowing he will go to Heaven.

THE NEW ODIN.

AN ORPHIC EVANGEL FOR THE SONS OF LODE.

"Mel et lac sub lingua tua."—SOLOMON'S SONGS.

His eloquent lips blow beautiful Evangels
    Through the clear-sounding Trumpet of his love,
Making such music as doth please the ears of Angels,
    New Æons adding to the Seraph's glowing joys above.

To this great Orphic-Builder all the merits
    Of all the Cherubim are freely given ;
So that this Demiurgos here on earth inherits
    All the rich honors that await the good in Heaven.

This Christ-built Temple, full of God's great glory,
    Becomes to those high souls who live by love,
A Sanctuary whence the incense of sweet story
    Floats upward, like Auroral clouds, to Heaven above.

Living Star-crowned above th' Olympian thunder,
   His soul enjoys Eternity in Time—
Filling the unborn Ages with the same sweet wonder
   Which makes the Present marvel at his Eagle-flights sublime.

Writing his Golden Songs on silver pages,
   The poorest heart he doth with richest joys possess—
Saluting all the listening ears of all the Ages
   With the immortal Paradise of his own happiness.

The patient Shepherds, out in Fields Elysian,
   Watching their flocks by night in open skies—
Hear the loud Advent-Song before the Vision
   Of God's great Cloud of Angels burst upon their eyes.

The Wise-Men of the World then say to one another—
   " The Night is now far spent—DAY is at hand !"
This Man shall make Mankind like brother unto brother,
   Because God's Kingdom cannot come with Devils in the
     land !

By the clear-flowing Elims of God's Spirit,
   Watering the Palestine of Truth, he sits him down,
And, striking there his golden harp, he doth inherit,
   For his sweet Burdens of Unrest, an Angel's crown.

Out of his God-enchastened soul there sometimes sighest
   A Dove-like Sorrow-Song, but oftener flow
Those jubilant Choral Hymns unto the Highest,
   Whose deep Arcana God alone in Heaven can know.

But through the dark clouds of his soul's deep sorrows,
   Breaks the Aurora of a richer Day,—
Prophetic of those Halcyon bright To-morrows,
   Whose golden Noons shall never, never pass away.

TONTINE HOTEL, NEW HAVEN, December 22, 1851.

5*

CYGNE D'ITALIA.

Oh! santa Melodia!

I drink, bewildered with divine delight,
   Refreshing draughts out of thy soul's deep shining Well;
And walk, arrayed in robes of living white,
   Through Heaven's immortal Bowers of Asphodel,—
Translated on the pinions of the Dove,
Feeding on music from the honeyed lips of love.

New forms of Beauty thou didst in my soul awaken,
   New joys inspiring, such as Angels feel above,—
Like some tall Reed by winds from Eden shaken,
   My soul swayed, bent down by the music of thy love;
As one, when lifted suddenly from distress,
Falls at the Gates of God with too much happiness.

As when the Moon comes out upon the Hills of Heaven,
   And troubles Ocean with the presence of her light;
Did thy dear Beauty, when to me first given,
   Madden my spirit with an infinite delight—
As one who wanders through the Gate of Dreams,
Amid the Bowers of Bliss, beside Elysian streams.

Up to the Alpine Peaks of thy sweet song,
   My soul soared, singing, shouting while it soared,
Echoing the utterance of thy sweet Angelic tongue,
   Piling around Heaven's Gate the fountains that were
     poured
Out of thy soul in rivers of ecstatic fire—
Drowning the Archangel's songs to silence with thy heavenly
   Lyre.

For as the Lightnings strike out from the clouds cool rain,
   Refreshing, with their fall, the thirsting Earth;

So thou didst from our souls, with thy sweet strain,
    The tears of joy, expressive of thy heavenly worth—
The rosy richness of whose soft Aonian song
Unto Edenic chimes high up above th' Empyrean Realms
    belong.

Over the coral curve of thy sweet lips did roll
    A cascade of sweet song of spiritual fire,
Out of the fountains of thy rich immortal soul,
    Preaching of Beauty with an Angel's heavenly Lyre—
Where soft Persuasion, clad in robes of light,
Sat shedding odor from her wings of spotless white.

ALAMOTH;

OR,

THE SONG OF HIDDEN THINGS.

Thine own Evangels are divinest Revelations,
    And thou the Apotheosis of thy sweet Song!
Pour forth, Oh! SOUL! thy heavenly ministrations,
And let thy rivers of rich honey flow out all night long!

Reveal to us the Vision thou art seeing
    At heaven's high Gates, in rapture-tones sublime,
Through the Apocalypse of thy divinest being—
Quenching with God's sky-rivers all the thirsting souls of Time.

Give us some history of that high-up YONDER,
    Above the Stars—where thunders never roll—
Where dwell the souls for whom our own grow fonder,
As, year by year, we grow more like them here in soul!

Oh! God! lift up that Heaven-concealing Curtain
    Which hides the HOLY OF HOLIES from our eyes;
And let us see, that we may know for certain,
If those we loved here most wait for us in the skies!

Yon Starry Scripture tells but half the story,
Shining in splendor on the outward walls above—
(Like Angels camped upon the Fields of Glory—)
They show us not God's face, nor those dear souls we love!

Show us, dear LORD! reveal to us more clearly
The glories that await us there on high;
And those fond souls we loved on earth so dearly,
And we will weep no more, but wait with patient joy to die!

THE CHAPLET OF PALMS.

An Elegy composed on the death of HUNTINGTON LYMAN a beautiful little boy, who died, very suddenly, on the 10th of February, 1852, of Scarlet Fever.

"Why stand ye here gazing up into Heaven?"—BIBLE.

Softly clasp to your bosom
This sweet bud gone to blossom
Up in Heaven—you must lose him—
You must lose what you thought far too pretty to die!
Oh! more tremblingly press him—
With soft kisses caress him—
Calling God down to bless him—
Who now waits there to crown him with glory on high.

In the Angel's embraces—
See! he smiles in their faces!
To the Heavenly Places
He now soars up aloft like some Dove from its nest;
Father—mother cease sighing—
For his soul is undying—
Unto God he goes flying—
Where the wicked cease troubling—the weary find rest.

Bear him up, ye blest Spirits !
Into Heaven ! for he merits
Those rewards he inherits
From his Father, his Saviour—for, oh ! he was good !
Oh ! receive him, blest Saviour !
For his Christ-like behaviour—
Lying low in his grave here,
Like the frost-bitten lily unblown in the bud !

As he onward advances,
See the Angels in trances,
With the bright Excellencies,
Coming downward to meet him with Palms in their hands !
Now they press through the Portal
Of the Jasper-walled Court all,
With the Garlands immortal,
There to crown his fair brow where his Saviour now stands !

From the odorous abysses
Of their lips full of blisses,
They now feed him on kisses,
Till he swoons away rapt with the riches divine—
While with rapture ecstatic—
(Rich revealings emphatic—)
They pour Pæans pathetic
On his soul to salute him Christ's Cherub, as thine.

In that City whose whiteness
Far exceeds every brightness—
(Sunning God's infiniteness—)
Darkening whole Constellations of Suns with its shine—
Stand my children, all vestal,
At the Portals of crystal,
Raining songs most celestial
From their lips on his soul as they hail him divine !

These Elegiac Posies,
   Mixed with white leaves of roses,
    In his grave, ere it closes,
I will scatter, like snow, from my heart while it burns—
   As an emblem undying
   Of his mother's love crying
   For his body here lying—
Whose untimely decease she forever more mourns !

TONTINE HOTEL, NEW HAVEN, Feb. 12, 1852.

——❖——

PRIMO AMORE.

Where the amorous Winds deflowered
   The wild Roses in their bloom,
Whose sweet hearts were overpowered
   With the richness of perfume—
Through the Woodlands ever sunny,
   In the South-land far away,
Where the wild bees gather honey,
   We went wandering all the day—
   Wandering all the live-long day—
   Wandering, singing, all the day,
   In the South-land far away.

As the Moon will trouble Ocean,
   Though her face doth calmly shine;
So, my heart was all emotion,
   While contentment dwelt in thine.
For my sadness was the wanting
   Of that confidence in thee,
Which thy fond heart, early granting,
   Made this world like Heaven to me—
   While we wandered all the day—
   Wandered, singing, all the day,
   In the South-land far away.

As some calm, clear, azure river
   Clothes the banks it rolls between,
With soft verdure, which, forever,
   By its waves are kept so green;
So, thy love for me down-flowing
   In affection's river bright,
Greens my heart—(with passion glowing—)
   With the Spring of pure Delight—
   While we wander all the day—
   Wander, singing, all the day,
   In the South-land far away.

Oh! then, Dearest! never leave me,
   While my heart keeps true to thine;
For no grief can ever grieve me,
   If thine own prove true to mine;
And, through Woodlands ever sunny,
   In the South-land far away,
Where the wild bees gather honey,
   We will wander all the day—
   Wander all the live-long day—
   Wander, singing, all the day,
   In the South-land far away.

NEW YORK, May 10, 1842.

------✦------

FIRST LOVE.

Oh! what is the matter with my true love?
   Sing heigh-ho! heigh-ho!
Three times she sighed like the Turtle Dove—
   Sing heigh-ho! heigh-ho! heigh-ho!

The tear-drops stood in her deep blue eyes—
   Sing heigh-ho! heigh-ho!
Like an April rain in the sunny skies—
   Sing heigh-ho! heigh-ho! heigh-ho!

She laid her head on my panting breast—
  Sing heigh-ho! heigh-ho!
And my heart grew glad with her own unrest—
  Sing heigh-ho! heigh-ho! heigh-ho!

I clasped her then in my trembling arms—
  Sing heigh-ho! heigh-ho!
And crowned my soul with her matchless charms—
  Sing heigh-ho! heigh-ho! heigh-ho!

I laid mine own on her trembling cheek—
  Sing heigh-ho! heigh-ho!
And tried my lips—but I could not speak—
  Sing heigh-ho! heigh-ho! heigh-ho!

She lay on my breast, as she looked at me—
  Sing heigh-ho! heigh-ho!
Like a milk-white Ship on a rolling Sea—
  Sing heigh-ho! heigh-ho! heigh-ho!

She hid her face in her golden hair—
  Sing heigh-ho! heigh-ho!
And, in doing this, seemed to me more fair—
  Sing heigh-ho! heigh-ho! heigh-ho!

I moved the veil from her shining face—
  Sing heigh-ho! heigh-ho!
And sunned my soul in her matchless grace—
  Sing heigh-ho! heigh-ho! heigh-ho!

As a God his Nectar in glory sips—
  Sing heigh-ho! heigh-ho!
I sucked her soul through her smiling lips—
  Sing heigh-ho! heigh-ho! heigh-ho!

As Adam beheld in his Eve's fair eyes—
    Sing heigh-ho! heigh-ho!
The welcome that made all the world Paradise—
    Sing heigh-ho! heigh-ho! heigh-ho!

As an Angel freed from his body waits—
    Sing heigh-ho! heigh-ho!
For his soul to pass through the heavenly Gates—
    Sing heigh-ho! heigh-ho! heigh-ho!

As he then exults when he first gets in—
    Sing heigh-ho! heigh-ho!
To the Courts of God where there is no sin—
    Sing heigh-ho! heigh-ho! heigh-ho!

When he strikes his Harp of a thousand strings—
    Sing heigh-ho! heigh-ho!
With the smiles of God on his shining wings—
    Sing heigh-ho! heigh-ho! heigh-ho!

As the Angels welcome him home to bliss—
    Sing heigh-ho! heigh-ho!
So my soul first felt when I drew that kiss—
    Sing heigh-ho! heigh-ho! heigh-ho!

From the crystalline wells of her eyes of love—
    Sing heigh-ho! heigh-ho!
I drank what the Saints drink in Heaven above!
    Sing heigh-ho! heigh-ho! heigh-ho!

I asked her then if she would be mine?
    Sing heigh-ho! heigh-ho!
And she, smiling, said, " *I am thine! I'm thine!* "
    Sing heigh-ho! heigh-ho! heigh-ho!

Villa Allegra, Ga., April 10. 1849.

THE MARVEL OF ARABIA.

From the Arabic of Caab.

Thy sweet mouth is like some Garden
   Well inclosed with rosy bowers ;
Thy sweet lips, like Eden's Warden,
   Guarding it with swords of flowers—
More odorous than the Attar-Gul
Made of the Rose that won Bul-Bul.

Like the Cherubim that guarded
   Eden's Gates of Promise fair,
They now keep thy pure soul warded,
   Safe from every earthly care—
More odorous than the Attar-Gul
Made of the Rose that won Bul-Bul.

Watering this fair Eden vestal,
   With sweet rivulets of song,
Purling cascatelles of crystal
   Leaped the coral of her tongue—
More odorous than the Attar-Gul
Made of the Rose that won Bul-Bul.

Let their unsealed silence, oral,
   Into rapturous rivers roll,
Over cataracts of coral—
   Eden opens on my soul—
More odorous than the Attar-Gul
Made of the Rose that won Bul-Bul !

Her white breasts hang on her bosom
   Like Magnolias in the bud,
Side by side, about to blossom,
   Fairest ones in all the wood—
Like Angel's fruit, upon some heavenly Tree,
Growing in Eden, not to touch, but see.

Then the teeth of this fair daughter,
   Seen behind her lips divine,
Looked like bubbles of pure water
   Dancing on the top of wine ;
Eden's Opal walls were not more even—
Sparkling like the Pleiades of Heaven.

Fairer than the Moon when crescent,
   Was her oval forehead fair,
When no clouds in Heaven are present,
   And the sky looks very clear ;
Her breath more odorous than the Attar-Gul
Made of the Rose that won Bul-Bul.

Underneath her floor of crystal
   Trickled rivulets of song,
Lulling this fair virgin vestal
   Into slumber calm as long—
The Diamonds sparkling there so bright at even,
That night seemed day—but it is always Day in
     Heaven.

NEW HAVEN, July 8, 1850.

———❖———

LAMENT FOR MARY IN HEAVEN.

Death, the sweet sleep of the weary—
(Ah ! its pang is momentary—)
Thou dost feel it not, sweet Mary !
   In that dark, cold grave of thine !
Where thy body is reclining,
While thy soul above is shining—
(And mine own is left here pining—)
   As a Star in Heaven doth shine !
     Care Maria, vale !

Though thou art in Heaven above me,
Yet, on earth you used to love me ;
And this thought doth often move me,
   When my life is turned to wo !
When I think of thine in gladness,
All my soul is turned to sadness—
Goaded almost on to madness—
   That mine own cannot be so !
      Care Maria, vale !

For thy soul dwelt in thy features,
Thou most perfect of God's creatures !
As His Spirit dwells in Nature's—
   Now in Heaven among the blest !
While my soul is left here weeping
At the grave where thou art sleeping,
While the worms are on thee creeping—
   Would to God that I had rest !
      Care Maria, vale !

VILLA ALLEGRA, GA., June 10, 1842.

ORPHIC HYMN OF THE NEW JERUSALEM

Sing, at the Tomb of Joseph first began
The spiritual glory of the Son of Man,
Casting his body off, he there put on
God-robes of lightning brighter than the sun !

Covered with God's excessive glory bright,
He walked invisible to mortal sight—
Except to those whose eyes were couched to see
The blazing splendor of his Majesty !

He came unto the Ancient One of Days
To sit beside him on his throne always—
Riding in lightning-Chariot through high Heaven
Up to the throne that He to him had given.

He sits in centre of the BURNING ROW
Of those BRIGHT LAMPS OF GOD in glory now,
Singing, like Stars, around him while they shine,
A thunderous song in myriad choir divine.

As by the Angelic Convoy he was led
From Death to Life, (the First-born of the dead,)
So shall we rise, (the pledge by him being given)
In plenary glory from the grave to Heaven.

For all the Priesthood at his death was slain—
Killed—crucified—when he began to reign;
Doomed with his fond Disciples now to sup
No more till his great Kingdom was set up.

For in his Father's glory he arose,
Pulling down Death's dark throne upon his foes!
Planting his spiritual Kingdom there instead
Of the Old Law, which in the grave was laid.

For his Humanity was glorified
By that Divinity he cast aside—
(Emptying himself of glory to be Man)
Possest in Heaven before the world began.

These shining garments which to him were given,
Were those of which he was disrobed in Heaven—
Which he put on again when he arose
From Death, wherein he left his old grave-clothes.

Then in his God-like vestiture divine
He shone on earth as now in Heaven doth shine—
Bright as when Paul beheld him—GLORIOUS ONE!
Brighter than brightness of the noonday sun!

6*

For in Prophetic ecstacy of trance
He saw the Holy One's bright countenance
Beaming in brightness brighter than the Sun,
By which he knew it was the HOLY ONE!

And as those mortal robes in which he died,
When he arose from Death, were cast aside—
Putting on those primeval robes of light,
He wore in Heaven before his Father's sight—

So shall we cast our mortal robes away,
Putting on garments of Celestial Day,
Pure as the BODY OF HEAVEN in Heaven shall be,
Beside God's throne in immortality.

VILLA ALLEGRA, GA., July 8, 1842.

---✧---

ISRAFELIA.

Composed on hearing Jenny Lind sing in Castle Garden, N. Y.

" Cœlo venit aurea dextro."—MANILIUS.

They tell us that there was in Heaven above
    An Angel whose sweet heartstrings are a lute,＊
Who, when he doth dispart his lips of love,
    The Angels with their ravishment grow mute;
And the rapt Muses with their bowed heads pine
To see in him all that they thought their own by right divine.

They tell us, too, that there was once on high
    A Star, the brightest of the radiant Seven,
Which long ago departed from the sky,
    And either came on earth, or went to Heaven—
Leaving the Six sad Sisters to lament
The loss of that whose glory filled the firmament.

" ＊The Angel Israfel, who has the most melodious voice of all God's creatures."—SALES' KORAN.

This Angel, who was once in Heaven above,
    Whose living heartstrings are a lute ;
This Star which circled in the Courts of Love,
    For whose long absence now the rest are mute—
Is here on earth ! Queen of the radiant Seven !
The living Glory of the Six now left in Heaven !

This glorious Angel stooping from her sphere,
    A blessing from the Gods to mortals given—
Has come to lift us from this dark world here,
    Upon the wings of music into Heaven !
Now the rapt Muses with their bowed heads pine
To see in her all that they thought their own by right divine.

NEW YORK, January 10th, 1851.

————◈————

THE TREE OF HEAVEN.

The Rose that all are praising,
    Is the Rose that blooms for me—
Whom the Angels now are raising
    Over every other tree—
This is the Rose that blooms for me.

In the middle of God's Garden
    Grows this white celestial Tree,
And an Angel is the Warden
    Of the flowers that bloom for me
In this Eden on this Tree.

There she grows beside the River
    Of immortal life for me,
Where she towers aloft forever
    Over every other tree—
This is the Rose that blooms for me.

While the Breezes blow Evangels
  From the harp-like boughs for me,
She is tended by the Angels
  Over every other tree—
This is the Rose that blooms for me.

Like the Moon star-crowned at even—
  (But not half so white as she—)
Circled by the Swans of Heaven—
  Blooms this white Celestial Tree
In the Bowers of Bliss for me.

Thus the Rose that all are praising,
  Is the Rose that blooms for me,
Whom the Angels now are raising
  Over every other tree—
This is the Rose that blooms for me.

BOSTON, December 4, 1852.

———◆———

TO THE ONLY ONE.

"I crown thee, love!
I crown thee queen of me?"—FESTUS.

Swift as the fond mate to his Dove,
  My soul now flies to thee,
To place this new-born ROSE OF LOVE,
Pulled from Affection's Paphian Grove—
  Upon thy breast by me.

Thy voice is sweeter far to me
  Than either Harp or Lute;
For when those strings are touched by thee—
Thy lips are moved to melody—
  Each other voice is mute.

I have outwatched the sleepless stars
   While gazing upon thee;
And thou, my STAR! wert unawares,
Amid my many patient cares,
   Of being watched by me.

The Persian worships not the Sun,
   Because God dwells in light,
More true than I have ever done
Thy beauty, my CELESTIAL ONE!
   That cheers me day and night.

The Cave-nursed Plato felt Love's fire
   Burn in his heart like mine;
But not more pure was his desire,
When he to Heaven did first aspire,
   Than this fond soul for thine.

For that high burning love he felt,
   No name was ever given;
And no less object ever dwelt
Within my soul to make it melt
   With Passion's fires—than HEAVEN.

A VISION OF THE NIGHT.

I saw the bright Apocalypse
   Of God's Eternity;
With mild blue eyes, rapt Apollonian lips,
   He, smiling, looked on me.

Then suddenly came, as if down-hurled
   Out of great Memnon's lips of old,
Which, like an Earthquake, shook the world—
   These words of molten gold:

" *I am the* FATHER *of all Time—*
     All things were made by me !
The thunders of the Heavens sublime,
     *Are mine own voice—*ETERNITY *!* "

More glorious than the golden skies
     Of a thousand setting Suns,
Is the face of God unto him who dies
     In the hopes of the heavenly Ones !

VILLA ALLEGRA, GA., April 10th, 1836.

———�֎———

ISABEL.

" In the shades of bright Hoboken,
     By the Sybil's lonely well,
There I gave you this fond token,
Of the vows that then were spoken—
Vows that never have been broken
     But by thee, dear Isabel !

" Then you said to me, when sighing,
     You would always love me well ;
Then my soul, on thine relying,
Said the same dear thing, replying—
Now my soul to God is crying
     For redress, dear Isabel !

" In the shades of bright Hoboken,
     As the Angels know full well,
There our plighted vows were spoken—
There this wretched heart was broken !
Give me back the golden token
     Of my love, false Isabel !

" For you sailed the Hudson over
   To the Sybil's Holy well,
Where, by stealth, I did discover,
In the fields of dewy clover,
That you had another lover
   Whom you loved, dear Isabel !

" I have now the golden token
   Of the heart that loved too well !
By the lies that thou hast spoken—
By this trusting heart, now broken,
In the shades of bright Hoboken
   Thou shalt die, dear Isabel ! "

Then, beside the Hudson's water,
   By the Sybil's lonely well,
In his arms he quickly caught her,
Like Virginius did his daughter—
Virgin lamb for early slaughter—
   And there slew his Isabel !

" Now my soul is overladen
   With such grief as none can tell !
Smile upon me, heavenly maiden,
From the jasper groves of Aiden !
In the grave that thou art laid in
   I will lie, lost Isabel ! "

Then her lover, broken-hearted,
   As on earth she fiercely fell,
Through his heart his dagger darted,
When his soul to God departed !
Who, to die, that morning started
   From New York with Isabel !

MEMORIAL OF MY CHILDHOOD.

How sweet to remember the Oaks of my childhood,
  Whose cool, shady twilights were haunts of my youth;
Those tall, emerald Pine trees that waved in the Wildwood,
  Whose boughs, in the breeze, sang the music of Truth.
And oh! to remember the China Tree growing
  Beside the big road serpentining the State,
Where often I shot, with my Cross-bow, when snowing,
  The Robins that perched on the boughs near the Gate;
And shot with my Cross-bow—my Mulberry Cross-bow,
  The Robins that perched on the boughs near the Gate.

And oh! how delightful the clear. crystal waters
  Flowed sporting along through the wood-skirted Vale,
Where mother once walked with her dear little daughters,
  And combed down their dark, glossy locks in the gale.
How fondly I marched with my Cross-bow and arrows,
  That hung on my arm as I ambled along,
Where all the day long I have hunted the sparrows,
  And listened at eve to the Mocking-bird's song;
And shot with my Cross-bow—my Mulberry Cross-bow,
  The Robins that perched on the boughs near the Gate.

There are four sombre Oaks o'er the Well-top inclining,
  That Nature, in sport, planted out for a shade—
So near equidistant, with artful designing,
  That strangers believed them an artful Arcade.
'Twas there the old Scullion suspended the butter,
  While I, with my Cross-bow, sat high in the tree,
And shot at the Robins, while sister would mutter,
  And wistfully look through the boughs up at me;
And shot with my Cross-bow—my Mulberry Cross-bow,
  The Robins that perched on the boughs near the Gate.

Ah! then I was happy—with love overflowing—
    But knew not the value of pleasure by pain—
Till Grief's bitter frost nipped my Roses while blowing,
    And now I can never be happy again!
And oh! to remember that Dayspring of pleasure,
    Unmixed with the present reflection in pain,
Methinks it were well to look back on the Treasure,
    And strive all my life to procure it again;
And shoot with my Cross-bow—my Mulberry Cross-Bow,
    The Robins that perched on the boughs near the Gate.

How gladly I roved through the Suckle-gemmed Valley—
    The grove where the Wash-woman filled up her tank;
And stood by the Well in the green Oaky Alley,
    And turned down the old Cedar Bucket and drank.
But, farewell, ye Oaks, and the Trees of my Childhood,
    And all the bright scenes appertaining to joy—
I think of ye often away in this Wildwood,
    But never shall be as I was when a boy;
Nor shoot with my Cross-bow—my Mulberry Cross-bow,
    The Robins that perched on the boughs near the Gate.

TRANSYLVANIA UNIVERSITY, April 10, 1830.

———◈———

EUTHANASIA.

She died in meekness, like the noiseless lamb
    When slain upon the altar by the knife;
And lay reclining on her couch so calm,
    That all who saw her said she still had life;
And like the humming-bird that seeks the bower,
    But wings her swiftly from the place away—
Bearing the dew-drop from the fading flower—
    Her spirit wandered to the ISLE OF DAY.

7

She died in softness, like the Dorian flute
    When heard melodious on the hills at night—
When every voice but that loved-one is mute,
    And all the holy heavens above are bright.
And like the rain-bow of the sunny skies,
    (The dew-drop fillet of the brow of even,)
That blends its colors as the evening dies,
    Her beauty melted in the light of Heaven.

NEW YORK, October, 1837.

----- ❖ -----

ATALA'S PRAYER.

"ALAS! to die so young, when my heart is so full of love!"—CHATEAUBRIAND.

Abba ! when the morn is breaking
    Through the Portals of the sky,
And the dappled Fawns are waking
    In the REED-ISLES where they lie;
When the Roe-buck gazes wildly
    At the Hunter in the even,
And the milky Moon looks mildly
    From the azure depths of Heaven;
When the Turtle Doves are mourning
    In the ROSE-ISLES of the sea,
And the stars above are burning—
    Lift my spirit up to Thee !

Abba ! when the Fowls are laving
    In the Fountains far away,
Where the Purple Hills are waving
    In the Sunny Isles of Day;
When the Mocking-birds are singing
    By the river-banks at noon,
And the Violet-bells are springing
    From the Rosy-Hills in June;

When the Pigeons all are feeding
  On the beech-mast by the sea,
And my bosom shall lie bleeding—
  Lift my spirit up to Thee!

Abba! when the Reed is broken
  That has borne me up when young,
And the last sad word is spoken
  That shall tremble on my tongue;
When the Roe-buck comes to wander
  From the Green Hills far away,
And my breaking heart grows fonder
  For the Sunny Isles of Day;
When my Forest Home is taken,
  And the Stranger bids me flee;
Abba! call me, Thy Forsaken—
  Take my spirit home to Thee!

VILLA ALLEGRA, GA., March 13, 1835.

TO AVALON IN HEAVEN.

Son of the highest God! why should I weep
      Because of thee?
As well may some bright Shell beneath the deep
    Be troubled for the sighing Sea,
    As I be troubled now for thee—
      Son of the Highest God!

Son of the Highest God! I will not weep
      Because of thee—
But for myself alone! for does the Deep
Weep for the Shell? the Shell weeps for the Sea—
As thou, in Heaven, shouldst ever weep for me—
      Son of the Highest God!

VILLA ALLEGRA, GA., Sept. 10, 1848.

LORD BYRON'S DYING WORDS TO ADA.

"Save me, O God! for the waters have come in unto my soul."—PSALM LXII, 1.

The ball that wounds the mated dove
　Inflicts but little pain ;
But bitter is this shaft of love
　By which my soul is slain !
For he that trusts the broken reed,
　Shall feel it pierce for aye
The heart that must forever bleed—
　My little babe, good-bye !
　Good-bye, my love ! good-bye !
　My little babe, good-bye !

As dew-drops, pure and chaste as snow,
　In falling, may be changed ;
So hearts, oft chilled and racked by wo,
　Will soon become estranged !
The dog that meets with constant blows
　Will shun his master's eye,
And snap the hand that food bestows —
　My little babe, good-bye !
　Good-bye, my love ! good-bye !
　My little babe, good-bye !

Thy years are not enough to know
　The sorrows that await !
In Friendship's garb doth Envy go,
　To haunt thee, long and late !
Then task the vows that men may give,
　As future years roll nigh ;
For I am now too sick to live—
　My little babe, good-bye !
　Good-bye, my love ! good-bye !
　My little babe, good-bye !

And though mine eyes may never see
    Thy face on earth, my love!
Yet, God will fix some plan for me
    To meet my child above!
This consolation soothes my plaint,
    And cancels every sigh;
But now my heart doth burst!—I faint!—
    My little babe, good-bye!
    Good-bye, my love! good-bye!
    My little babe, good-bye!

OAK GROVE, GA., June 18, 1831.

——✿——

SONG TO UNA OF AUSTER.

My soul was lifted half way up to Heaven
    Upon the sweet tones of thy voice, dear Maiden!
Like some sweet golden Butterfly at even,
    Bright Angel of the Flowers! with lips dew-laden,
Floating on incense-clouds from out the Bowers of Aiden.

For thy celestial, joy-inspiring song
    Brought to my heart the Halcyon bright to-morrow,
Which, coming, thou didst ever there prolong—
    A Goshen of sweet peace which Heaven might borrow—
Where Joy forever dwelt—but where came never Sorrow.

Singing of young Love in the Eden Days,
    Which we, now, in the present time, call Olden,—
When all my heart was poured out in my Lays,
    Like perfume from the flowers when new unfolden—
When silver truths fell from thy lips in words all golden.

7*

For, as the Wind doth purify the sea,—
　　The rivers are kept pure by their own motion;
　So is my soul by thy sweet melody—
　　So is my heart by its own pure devotion,
Which flows to thee, sweet ONE! as rivers to the ocean.

　Here, underneath thy dark locks, let me rest
　　My pensive head upon the snow-white billow
　Of thine impassioned, love-distracted breast,
　　As calmly as the Swan upon the pillow
Of some clear, azure Lake beneath the Weeping Willow.

———◈———

THE HEAVENLY REAPER.

　　　The Moon, my love calls fickle,
　　　　Dawning upon our sight,
　　　Comes, with her silver sickle,
　　　　To reap the Heavens to-night.

　　　Sweeping the fields of azure,
　　　　Into her Opal wain
　　　She gathers her golden treasure
　　　　Of stars which **are** lucid grain.

———◈———

IONA.

　She came so faultless from the hands of God,
　　Her beauty seems now to embody all
　The rich perfections that in Eve abode
　　To make her what she was before the fall.

　Celestial beauty radiates from her face,
　　As from some Goddess, unto whom is given
　Those matchless attributes of perfect grace,
　　Whom mortals worship by the name of HEAVEN.

PAS D'EXTASE.

Like those sweet Cydonian Suckets
Hebe brings in crystal Buckets
    To the Gods in Heaven above,
When they drink, forever quaffing
    Fiery draughts of living wine—
Sometimes shouting, sometimes laughing
    With the heavenly bliss divine;
Was my soul made drunk with gladness—
Rapt with most exultant madness—
    Joy so sweet it turned to wo—
Drinking down thy songs of sweetness
From thy heart's divine completeness,
    As if Heaven should overflow;
Like the Angel's heavenly laughter
Which the Gods go sighing after—
    Such as Gods alone can know;
Or the rapture of deep anguish
    Of some saintly soul when dying,
On his death-bed left to languish—
    Unto God forever crying—
When, amid his desolation,
Comes the news of his salvation,
    And his soul ascends up flying
Into Heaven with exultation—
    Like the Angels on the Ladder
Up from Bethel-plain at even;
    So my soul clomb gladder, gladder,
On the rounds of song to Heaven—
    Piled in incense from thy bosom,
Like the odor, late at even,
    From some Eden fresh in blossom,
When the world looks white as Heaven!

New York ; p:il 10, 1850.

SONG.

If you break the smallest link
  In the softest earthly chain—
(Save the one of which I think—)
  You may mend it oft again;
But the heart that once is riven,
  Oh! it cannot mended be!
For the chain was made in Heaven
  That now binds my soul to thee!

If you rob the turtle's nest
  Of her little ones, she tries
All the next day to find rest
  With her pinions in the skies;
And, alas! wherever driven,
  She is willing there to be,
Just because she has no Heaven,
  Like my soul, love! without thee!

THE CONFESSION.

Dear Lady! why sigh you so?
    "Say, why? say, why?"
My heart is opprest with wo,
The cause of thy grief to know!
    Oh! reply! *do* reply!
Have I wronged you? ye answer, No!
Then why are ye troubled so?
    "Say, why? say, why?"
"My heart is not burthened with wo,
  But with joy, that my tears now flow—
    Yet, I sigh! yet, I sigh!"

Dear Lady ! why weep you so ?
    " Say, why ? say, why ? "
My heart is opprest with wo,
The cause of thy grief to know !
    Oh ! reply ! *do* reply !

Are ye orphaned ? ye answer, No !
Then why are you weeping so ?
    " Say, why ? say, why ? "
" The reason that my tears now flow,
Is, because I do love you so !
    And must have you or die !
    I must have you or die !"

ALMA.

Blacker than the Blackbird's bill,
    Was her raven hair ;
Whiter than snow upon Ida's Hill,
    Was her forehead fair :
Like Ivory of Corinth her milk-white hand,
Her lips were like Rubies from Samarcand.

Softer than the April skies,
    When the sun goes down,
Suffused with the sunset's dyes,
    Were her eyes of brown ;
Like the Lioness', lazy, their hazle hue,
Or the Autumn leaf in the morning dew.

Fairer than the full-orbed Moon,
    Star-crowned, at even,
Sitting, in her highest Noon,
    On the Hills of Heaven ;
Melting my soul with her smiles of love,
Like the Moon melts the night in the Heavens above.

Whiter than the milk-white Swan
   On some crystal stream ;
Like the full blanc Moon at dawn
   By the Sun's tinct changed to cream ;
As wise as the Serpent—as meek as the Dove—
And, though living on earth, seemed in Heaven above.

DARK IS MY SOUL WITHOUT THEE.

Dark is my soul without thee,
   Light of my earliest love !
But think not that I doubt thee,
Though flatterers fawn about thee ;
   For if thou faithful prove,
   The Angels out of Heaven above
Will come down in this dark world to caress thee,
And with their lips of love forever bless thee.

Bright was my soul beside thee,
   Moon of my life's dark night !
But think not that I chide thee ;
Because such dark clouds hide thee,
   Drinking thy soul's sweet light—
   For if thou shine on them aright,
Angels from Heaven will come down to caress thee,
And with their lips of love forever bless thee.

Rich is my soul in pleasure,
   Anchored in thy deep love ;
Then let no earthly treasure,
Though proffered without measure,
   Cause thee to faithless prove ;
   For then no Angels from above
Would ever come down softly to caress thee,
Or with their lips of love forever bless thee.

VILLA ALLEGRA, GA., August 1, 1849.

BOAT-SONG.

On the soft flowing wave of that beautiful river
  By the light of the Moon we went sailing along;
While the Stars, like thy harp-strings, in Heaven seemed to quiver
  In delight to thy touch as my soul to thy song—
      Thy song, love! thy song!
While the Stars, like thy harp-strings, in Heaven seemed to quiver
In delight to thy touch, as my soul to thy song.

On the love-lighted wave of that river we glided,
  Like the young crescent Moon on the calm ether-sea;
When her Chariot of light through the Heavens is guided
  By one lone little Star, like my soul, love! by thee—
      By thee, love! by thee!
When her Chariot of light through the Heavens is guided
By one lone little Star, like my soul, love! by thee!

1836.

——✿——

CHANT D'AMOUR.

The ewe-sheep knows her little lamb
  Amid ten thousand little lambkins playing;
The lambkin knows her tender voice of balm
  Amid ten thousand other sheep, when straying:
So does my soul, amid ten thousand, see
The one ten thousand times most dear to me.

I lie down like the Marigold,
  At sunset, when I should be sleeping;
And rise up with him, as he doth unfold
  ' His petals to the sun with weeping;
Because thou art the sun that shines for me,
And I the flower that only blooms for thee.

As longs the Day's-eye for the light,
    When Earth in the embrace of Night is lying;
So does my soul, that blossoms at thy sight,
    Droop when the presence of its day is dying ;
Because the only Sun that shines for me,
Gives life unto the flower that blooms for thee.

----*----

THE PLACE WHERE I WAS BORN.

You may talk of those green grassy Isles,
    Which the Tritons have strewn with their coral,
Which the day-god impregns with his smiles,
    Where the seasons forever are floral ;
Of the vales of the rich Arcady,
    Where the evening is just like the morn ;
But the prettiest place in the world for me
    Is the cottage where I was born—
Where my father's dear children were born—
In the soft sunny South, where my parents were born.

You may talk of the bright Cyclades
    Which oasis the deserts of Ocean—
The three fairest Nymphs that inhabit the seas
    Which the moon keeps forever in motion ;
Of that BEAUTIFUL LAND far beyond the sea,
    Where the evening is just like the morn ;
But the prettiest place in the world for me
    Is the cottage where I was born—
Where my father's dear children were born—
In the soft sunny South, where my parents were born.

You may talk of those Gardens of Gul,
    Where the maidens make Cupid their treasure,
Where the zephyrs bear Venus at full
    Of the moon to the ISLANDS OF PLEASURE ;

Of that BEAUTIFUL LAND, far beyond the sea,
 Where the evening is just like the morn ;
But the prettiest place in the world for me,
 Is the cottage where I was born—
Where my father's dear children were born—
In the soft sunny South, where my parents were born.

THE INVITATION.

(A CUP OF NECTAR FOR THE LIPS OF LOVE.)

O ! come away, my gentle one !
 At midnight come to me,
And rest upon my breast alone,
 In moonlight by the sea.
The Moon shall hear each tender tone,
 The Stars above shall see
Thee lie upon my breast alone,
 In moonlight by the sea.
 Then come, dear one ! to me,
And lie upon my breast alone
 In moonlight by the sea.

O ! come again, my darling love !
 And meet me when thine eyes
Give glory to the stars above,
 And meekness to the skies.
At night alone should love be heard,
 And thou alone with me,
To dwell upon each whispered word
 In moonlight by the sea.
 Then come, dear love ! to me,
And dwell upon each whispered word
 In moonlight by the sea.

8

O ! come again, my dearest love !
　　When every thought is deep,
And meet me ere the stars above
　　Have sung the moon to sleep.
Say—will you come ! O ! tell me, Sweet !
　　Say, will you come to me ?
For, O ! it is such joy to meet
　　In moonlight by the sea !
　　Say—will you come to me ?
For, O ! it is such joy to meet
　　In moonlight by the sea !

VILLA ALLEGRA, GA., June 8, 1836.

------◈------

PERIA PERSICA.

Thy lips are Beauty's Ruby Mines,
Sweeter far than Eglantines ;
Conserve of roses mixed with cream,
Bliss of which the Gods might dream ;
The laughing rose-bud of the heart,
Love's tropic sun doth now dispart.
A kiss from those sweet lips of thine,
Intoxicates the soul like wine—
Sweeter, in the dews of speech,
Than the nectar of the peach.
Thy mouth is like the Signet on
The Jeweled-Ring of Solomon—
Where Cherub, soft persuasion lies,
Like Eve embowered in Paradise ;
A Casket full of pearly Gems
Kept pure for Venus' Diadems ;
A fountain from whose sweetness springs
All the joys the Poet sings—
Whose Syren tongue, with artless art,
Was the sweet thief that stole my heart.

THE ANGEL'S WHISPER.

By the sweet, tender smiles on thy countenance stealing,
  Now dimpling thy cheeks more than Heaven to me;
I know by the light of their heavenly revealing,
  That the dear little angels are whispering to thee—
      Are whispering, are whispering to thee—
I know by the light of their heavenly revealing,
  That the dear little angels are whispering to thee.

Like two violets bedewed in the light of the morning,
  Are thy mild, tender eyes turned in gladness to me;
By their soul-lighted azure thus rapturously burning,
  I know that the Angels are whispering to thee—
      Are whispering, are whispering to thee—
By their soul-lighted azure thus rapturously burning,
  I know that the Angels are whispering to thee.

Ah! nothing less pure than that saintly emotion
  Now thrilling thy pure little heart so for me,
Could inspire me to feel with such rapturous devotion,
  That the dear little Angels are whispering to thee—
      Are whispering, are whispering to thee—
Could inspire me to feel with such rapturous devotion,
  That the dear little Angels are whispering to thee.

Thy soft, lily-lips, dyed with roses, resemble—
  Thus cooingly, wooingly calling to me—
Two rose-leaves that in the soft breezes now tremble,
  Because the dear Angels are whispering to thee—
      Are whispering, are whispering to thee—
Two rose-leaves that in the soft breezes now tremble,
  Because the dear Angels are whispering to thee.

Like the Moon newly born in the soft azure bosom
    Of Heaven, art thou lying in thy cradle by me;
As white as the lily new-blown into blossom—
    Because the dear Angels are whispering to thee—
        Are whispering, are whispering to thee—
As white as the Lily new blown into blossom,
    Because the dear Angels are whispering to thee.

———◈———

BESSIE BELL.

Luz de mi Alma.

Do you know the modest Maiden,
    Pretty, bonny BESSIE BELL,
Queen of all the flowers of Aiden,
    Whom my heart doth love so well?
Ah! her eyelids droop declining
    On her soft cerulean eyes,
Like an unbought Beauty's, pining
    For the Harem's Paradise.

All her soul seemed full of blisses—
    All her heart seemed full of love—
Which she rained on me in kisses,
    Like Heaven manna from above.
Sought, the young Fawn in her wildness
    Is not wilder in the Dell;
Unapproached, the Dove in mildness
    Is not mild as BESSIE BELL.

Like the sweetest of Heaven's singers,
    ISRAFEL about his Lord,
Music smote her lily-fingers
    From her Heavenly Heptachord.

You should know this modest Maiden,
    Pretty, bonny BESSIE BELL,
Queen of all the Flowers of Aiden,
    Whom my heart doth love so well.

Like some sorrowing soul atoning
    For her sins with sobbing sighs—
Wasting, wailing, melting, moaning
    Out her heart in agonies;
Sang this saintly modest Maiden,
    Pretty, bonny BESSIE BELL,
Queen of all the Flowers of Aiden,
    Whom my heart doth love so well.

Like the psychical vibration
    Of the BUTTERFLY'S soft wings,
Dallying with the rich CARNATION—
    Played her fingers with the strings.
Israfelian in its dearness—
    All her heart's deep love to tell—
Bell-like, silver in its clearness,
    Fell the voice of BESSIE BELL.

Like some ruby Rose exhaling
    Its perfume upon the air,
Her sweet lips kept ever wailing
    Out her soul in words of prayer.
Do you know this modest Maiden,
    Pretty, bonny BESSIE BELL,
Whose sweet heart is overladen
    With such love as none can tell?

A fierce thrill of deep devotion
    Then vibrated through my heart,
Broken into rapt emotion
    By the magic of her Art.

8*

How I love this modest Maiden,
   Pretty, bonny BESSIE BELL,
Queen of all the Flowers of Aiden—
   None on earth can ever tell.

VILLA ALLEGRA, GA., April 1?, 1846.

————◆————

TOHOO VABOHOO.

All things were changed !—the mighty earth
   Grew tremulous with fear !
Heaven's thunders, as the stars went forth,
   Shook each one from its sphere !
Earth had no speech—Heaven had no ear—
   No word was spoken—heard !
All Nature trembled, dumb with fear,
   Waiting upon the Lord !

Time's grave was darkness !—every spot
   Was filled with nothing—blight
Was on the face of Nature—not
   A star lit Heaven that night !
The Nations now were dumb !—the wars
   Were at an end—the strife
Of Empires !—Death, from out Hell's bars,
   Looked lean for want of life !

There was no world but Heaven !—no eye
   To see, if there had been
Aught to have gazed upon !—the sky
   Stood everywhere set in
The circle of the Eternal Years,
   A concave of pure nought—
Stretching like nothing first appears
   To man absorbed in thought,

But over this—above this night—
  This gloom encircled by
The will of God—was one bright light
  Filling Eternity !
It was the smile of God !—it shone
  And lit that BLEST ABODE ;
And all who gathered round the throne
  Beheld the face of God !

MIDDLETOWN, CONN., April 8, 1839.

———✤———

INVOCATION TO SPRING.

As one but late in love
Longs for his mistress, so my soul for thee
  Pines with impatience !   Come, then, from above,
Bright Angel of the Sun ! come down to me,
And clothe the bare boughs of the trees with buds,
And wake the song-birds in the solitudes !

As the parched traveler, in
His hour of thirst, pants for the cooling streams,
  So does my soul for thee !   The earth, fair queen,
Longs for the healing of thy heavenly beams,
That Winter may be melted from her reign,
And streams, now frozen, loosed to flow again.

Come to the wintry groves,
And fringe the bare boughs with the green leaves bright ;
  And tune the voices of the turtle-doves
To coo thy welcome with divine delight—
Call back the swans that have been absent long,
And make the birds resume their last years' song.

As Winter to the Earth—
Freezing the streams which fertilize her breast,
　　Muffling their music as they wanton forth,
So that their banks are left like one distrest,
Barren of verdure, cold as cold can be—
So is the frost of my despair to me!

　　　　O! raise up from the grave
Of Winter, flowers that have been nipt by frost!
　　And, from the seeds the winds have sown, repave
The world with those that seemed, but were not, lost!
Thou art their Saviour—they rely on thee—
But who shall ever bring my lost to me?

　　　　A balm is in the air—
A vernal freshness in the odorous breeze;
　　A living greenness on the hills long bare;
As on the bare boughs of the ghostly trees,
Changing their aspect, as on cheeks once dead,
A soft, reviving hue steals, faintly red.

　　　　The warm breath of the South,
Laden with perfumes from the odorous flowers,
　　Like blessings whispered from some loved one's mouth,
In love, steals balmy over these bare bowers,
Whose boughs are just beginning to put forth
Young buds, to match the green down on the earth.

　　　　Thy smiles begin to swell
The young buds on the boughs—soon they will burst,
　　And open in full bloom, of " tender smell,"
And quench, with honey-dew, the young bee's thirst;
And lace, with tassels of green leaves, the limbs
Which shade the lake whereon the young duck swims.

The green blades of the grass
Lean over on the margin of the brook,
 And on themselves, beneath, in its clear glass,
Shadowed at noontide, ever tireless look;
While their green banks above, whereon they grow,
Seem resting on their images below.

  The golden humming-bird,
At intervals, among the blossoms flits,
 Chirping, as soft its lulling wings are heard—
Swift-darting, glinting back the sun in fits—
Humming caresses to each flower it meets,
While rifling it of all its odorous sweets.

  The crystal-shining pond
Is speckled with the sun-clouds in the sky,
 Which, though above, seem in its depths beyond,
All images of those that float on high;
As if two skies, to make it blest, were given—
One in the lake, the other up in heaven.

  A golden tinge now lies
Spread on the surface of yon crystal lake
 Placid as one in death; while all the skies,
Seen in its mirror which no breeze doth break,
Are glowing with the flush of day, which shines
More golden—orange now—as he declines.

  O! as from death they rise,
With all the freshness of their former bloom,
 When summoned by our Maker to the skies,
So shall our bodies from the silent tomb—
Immortal—never more to die.   Then, Spring,
 I will of an immortal Summer sing!

BYRON.

"Most wretched men
Are cradled into Poetry by wrong:
They learn in suffering what they teach in song."—SHELLEY.

He was Humanity's incarnate wail—
Wasting away his soul in one sad tale;
The living Type of Truths that shall prevail
Long after individual power shall fail.

Perched on the cloud-crowned altitude sublime
Of Nature's Alps, Jove's Eagle, in his prime,
Heard the loud cataract of the stream of Time,
Breaking in thunder over shoals of crime.

Self-exiled from his native land, his flight
Was towards Italia, Land of Pure Delight!
Whence to the sun he turned his eagle-sight,
Striking his golden harp with hands of might.

Then, like God's angel in the sun, he stood,
Pouring his soul out in one bitter flood
Of sorrow, writing, with his own heart's blood,
The Funeral Song of England's selfish brood.

Singing the Funeral Song of his own caste,
He wrote the Epitaph of all the Past—
Refusing with his own class to be classed—
Dying in exile at the very last!

Archangel-like, he looked in God's own face,
Whose features in lakes, mountains he did trace—
Nature, God's symbol, with unstudied grace,
With child-like trust, did he in joy embrace.

He raised the golden cup up to his lips
Of life's ignoble pleasures—now he sips!
As when the moon into the sun's orb dips,
His cherub soul is turned to an eclipse!

For, wearied. with the emptiness of life,
He sought this respite from his bitter grief—
This transient Lethe of his soul's deep strife
With which his Eagle-heart was ever rife.

But when the battle-cry of Freedom fell
Out of the soul of Greece, (his own death-knell !)
The same sweet cup he seemed to love so well,
Was dashed to fragments on the rock of Hell !

For when Greece, from her lofty mountains, heard
The soul-uplifting song of this great bird,
She shouted " LIBERTY !"—the last sweet word
That fell from out his Heavenly Heptachord.

Beside God's throne, Jove's Eagle, in his prime,
Hears the loud cataract of the stream of Time,
Breaking in thunder over shoals of crime,
Die in the Anthems of the Heavenly clime.

———✦———

TO FLORENCE IN HEAVEN.

"A Seraph in the realms of rest."—ROGERS.

Thou wert to me in this dark world so lonely,
    Smiling upon me with those eyes of love,
Like some bright star which shines upon me only—
    So bright no other seems to shine above.

As fades that star whose looks me home have lighted
    To joys as pure as its own beams divine—
Leaving me here alone on earth benighted ;
    So faded from my soul that face of thine !

As some lone traveler, by the night misguided,
    Misseth his path when his bright star is gone—
So left, alas ! by death from thee divided,
    My soul now wanders through this world alone !

VILLA ALLEGRA, GA., Dec. 12, 1842.

WORDS TO THE UNWISE.

"My People are destroyed for lack of Knowledge."—HOSEA.

Ye have no echoes in your souls
　　Of Heaven's celestial music-tones ;
Such Angel-language never rolls
　　Out of your hearts, ye simple ones !

For thy distraction of the heart,
　　There is no earthly Anodyne ;
Such sickness baffles human art,
　　Though it resemble the Divine.

As on the opening flowers at even
　　Descends the ever freshening dew,
Has God poured on thee out of Heaven
　　The unerring instinct of the True.

The experience of Earth's early youth—
　　The foregone Ages—all combine
To teach thee that undying Truth
　　Which made even Christ on earth Divine.

If thou wouldst live in endless youth—
　　Like Angels through Eternity—
Be thou the unembodied Truth,
　　And thou shalt never, never die.

Fathom the depths of thine own soul,
　　And thou wilt others understand ;
Who knows himself, will have the whole
　　Of human Knowledge at command.

VILLA ALLEGRA, GA., Aug. 10, 1846.

VIGIL OF SORROW.

In the sweet language of that heavenly Hymn,
  I cry out, in my sorrows, day by day;
So, that, all night mine eyes with tears are dim—
  Come, Angels! help me roll this rock away!

Not only are his grave-clothes lying there,
  But his dear body, also, wrapped in clay!
I still can hear no answer to my prayer—
  No Angel comes to roll the rock away!

Like some sweet lily-bud before its bloom,
  Waiting the advent of the God of Day—
His little body lies here in the tomb,
  For Angels' hands to roll the rock away.

Now his dear father at the grave-door stands,
  Striving to move it—but it still will stay;
It is too heavy for these mortal hands—
  Angels alone can roll the rock away!

The red clay, lying on his coffin-lid,
  Makes mountains on my soul of grief to-day;
Not to be moved, till, as for Christ they did,
  The Angels come to roll the rock away.

As Winter waits for Spring to come again,
  And robe her nudeness in her green array—
Long have I waited here on earth, in vain,
  For Angels' hands to roll the rock away!

Though he has now been dead for five long years,
  Yet, I cannot persuade myself to-day
That God will not yet furnish, for my tears,
  Some Angel's hands to roll the rock away.

9

For every time I look upon his grave,
   I feel that he is living here to-day;
For surely, were he dead, I would not crave
   An Angel's hands to roll this rock away.

Here will my soul these patient vigils keep,
   Green as the Myrtle on his grave to-day;
Waiting in sorrow that can never sleep,
   Some Angel's hands to roll this rock away!

Not till that blessed hour, when I shall see
   Him, face to face, in Heaven's immortal day—
Will this great boon be granted unto me—
   Some Angel's hands to roll this rock away!

VILLA ALLEGRA, GA., Oct. 10, 1848.

———✦———

SOPHIA.

"The wise shall inherit glory."—BIBLE.

What is wisdom, but the surely
   Knowing of ourselves aright,
Whereby we, reflected purely,
   Angels see in our own light.

Be thyself thine own Ideal,
   Great Incarnate Soul of love!
If thou wouldst possess the Real
   Here on earth of Heaven above.

In the Eternal Temple bowing
   Of the wide world humbly bow,
Thanking God for thus bestowing
   On thee power to worship so.

Let each act of thine betoken
    All the Truths you would declare;
And each Truth, whenever spoken,
    Be exprest in words of prayer.

By thy soul's serenest travail,
    Thou shalt into being bring
Truths which no one can unravel
    But the Truths which thou dost sing.

Wisdom is from God—no evil
    Can from Wisdom ever flow;
All our ignorance from the Devil,—
    And, from Ignorance, all our woe!

Dawn of Heaven's Eternal Morning!
    Break upon our raptured sight!
All our souls with Truth adorning—
    Chase away the world's dark night.

OAK GROVE, GA., August 10, 1842.

————✤————

THE DYING NIGHTINGALE.

"Oh! miserable me!"—CALDERON.

Birds of the wilderness!
Ye woodland choristers of many dyes!
Wake ye not in the night at my distress
    Poured forth more deep than all your melodies?
How can ye sleep beneath the boundless sea
Of my soul's grief poured forth in melody?

        Why was to my heart given
A more impassioned fulness than to thine?
Why should it be by its own richness riven—
    Doomed, by its own sweet eloquence, to pine—
Distracting thus the silence of the night
With its deep, fiery, mournful undelight?

Night is the time for sleep—
  By day-time all the other minstrels sing—
While, for its own deep love, my heart must weep
  Itself away in song—as with the spring
Faileth the river—that it cannot find
One mate, on earth, for its earth-hating mind!

  Oh! why was it my fate
  To find, for my impassioned soul, relief
Only by pouring out disconsolate
  And bitter strains, to ease my heart's deep grief?
For, as the streams of their rough shoals complain,
So does my heart of grief in this sad strain!

  Where is the friend to grant
  Requital for my grief in this deep strain?
Some *faithful* friend to share in my complaint,
  And half-partake with me its bitter pain?
Mute is my mate—though drowned beneath the flood
Of my soul's grief poured forth in solitude!

  Yes—mute is my soul's mate!—
  She cannot sing to share with me this strain,
Through which my soul tells of its bitter fate—
  Whose doom, in this dark world, is to complain!
No, she is silent—silent, on yon bough,
As death itself—mute as my own soul now!

1846.

————◆————

SONG TO THE POPPY.

Flower of sweet oblivion! take my soul
  To the dark wilderness of silent sleep,
Where soft, Lethean waters ever roll,
  And lull it into slumber calmly deep.

Let thy calm shadow rest upon me there,
    And bring me dreams of brighter worlds than this—
Let thy faint fragrance be mine atmosphere,
    And feed my soul with dreams of heavenly bliss.

Lead me where Sorrow, in the arms of Peace,
    Like some sweet child upon its mother's breast—
May draw the milk of joy, no more to cease,
    And, drinking, find therein eternal rest.

New York, July 10, 1842.

----&----

URANOTHEN.

Beneath the shelter of mine own dear home,
    I lay, one night, when all had gone to rest,
When, presently, there seemed from Heaven to come
    An Angel, telling me that she was blest.

The radiance from the light of her swift wings,
    Melted the moonlight as she came from rest,
Whose presence glorified all earthly things—
    Making them Heaven—telling me she was blest.

There was no sound—even Silence, by the breeze
    Of her odorous breath, was soothed to rest;
When, in the moonlight, underneath the trees,
    She came from Heaven—to tell me she was blest.

All things grew silent—voiceless—dumb as death—
    In awe of that dear being Heaven-possest—
My soul was speechless—when her Eden breath
    Parted her lips to tell me she was blest.

9*

The coming of her light-ensandaled feet,
    Star flowers upon the bloomless earth imprest;
Whose breath, with fragrance, made the air replete—
    My soul with joy—telling me she was blest.

The Cherubimic-truths which thrilled my ear
    The night's soft stillness with such joy imprest,
The mysteries of the grave were all made clear—
    Heaven was revealed—showing me she was blest.

Her beauty put out all things, as the sun
    Puts out the stars—of brighter light possest—
For heavenly Day came with that HEAVENLY ONE
    From Heaven above, to tell me she was blest.

She came so near me that she touched my soul—
    Her radiant hand sent rapture through my breast—
Which made the warm tears down my pale cheeks roll—
    She came from Heaven to tell me she was blest.

The sweet, dew-music of her rose-lips fell
    Soft on my heart's parched leaves by grief opprest,
More nectarous than the mystic Hydromel
    To Jove—wherewith she told me she was blest.

As light is rayed out from some star at even,
    Pensive within the chambers of the West,—
So was her glory, as she came from Heaven,
    In spiritual fire, to tell me she was blest.

As the God-praising music of the spheres
    Thrills audibly the Ether's hyaline breast;
So thrilled she my fond heart, with song, to tears,
    Which overflowed to know that she was blest.

The hyaline wavelets of her voice of love
   Rose on the soundless ether-seas calm breast;
Amid the interstarry realms above,
   To God in Heaven, telling me she was blest.

Her incense-voice, now echoing round the throne,
   Has left me here on earth so dispossest—
Wailing for that lost melody alone—
   I know no joy but this—*that she is blest.*

As God leans down from Heaven to earth to hear
   The Angel-music of man's heart opprest;
So leans she out of Heaven her gracious ear
   To hear me sing—*she told me she was blest.*

Silence, the mother of all sounds, grew mute
   To hear my heart beat joy within my breast,
As from her spirit-tongue, (her soul's sweet lute,)
   The music fell to tell me she was blest.

The Angel-gladdening music of the spheres,
   Singing the Cycles of her soul at rest,
Through the Great Sabbath of the Eternal Years—
   Echoes the Song that told me she was blest.

The luminous Huntress of the desert night,
   Haunting the Earth with her swift stars, exprest
With her cold voice, the infinite delight
   She felt to hear her tell me she was blest.

The radiance from the light of her swift wings
   Melted the moonlight as she went to rest;
For, as the snow-white Dove from earth upsprings,
   So went she back to Heaven among the blest.

VILLE ALLEGRA, GA., April 8, 1842.

SERENADE.

The Stars with their scinctilant splendor
    Of laughter bright,
Burn down through the deep blue tender
    With diamond light;
While the Heavens come down to surrender
    Their Crown to the Night—
    Bright Crown to the Night—
    Bright beautiful Crown to the Night.

The clouds with their soft silver fleeces
    Pavilion the Moon,
While the odors that float on the breezes
    Make Eden of June;
While my soul in its sorrow increases—
    Oh! come to me soon!
    Come down to me soon!
    Come down from thy home to me soon!

She looks with her eyes of azure
    Through all the night,
And they shed on the gloom such pleasure
    It makes all bright;
While the Heavens with their music make measure
    To my delight—
    My new-born delight—
    My new-born, divinest delight.

Like some Pyramid built up forever,
    Beginning with Time—
Out of beauty on beauty piled ever
    In utterance sublime—
Towering Heaven-ward, reaching it never—
    I will build me with rhyme—
    Build with melphonic rhyme—
An Epic of Jewels so set as to rhyme—
An Epic of Diamonds with Rubies for rhyme.

New Haven, August 1, 1851.

TO THE ROSE OF SONG.

Sweet rose-bud in the garden of pure song!
  As from the unfolding of young leaves arise
Sweet fragrance, which has lain therein so long;
  So, from thy parted lips, thy melodies,
In sweet perfume, now, flowing, make around
My soul an odorous ocean of sweet sound.

Sultana of my soul! the live-long night
  I heard thy brook-like voice, (still murmuring,)
Wave round my thoughts with deluge-like delight—
  Greening my heart with an immortal Spring
Of Heavenly pleasure; as the vales by rain
Are clad in verdure; Lady! sing again!

------◆------

TO THE MAID OF MANY SONGS.

Out of the ashes of the joyful fire
That has consumed me—(my funeral pyre—)
Out of the living death that I now die,
Listening to hear thy Heaven-revealing melody—
As one just risen from the midnight tomb
To flourish, after, in immortal bloom—
A new-born Phœnix—I arise! arise!
And soar up, shouting, through the echoing skies!
Instinct with all the joys to Angels known,
I rise rejoicing round the heavenly throne!
But now I die! I die again with bliss!
Swooning away with too much happiness—
That pierces through my heart into my brain—
Listening, entranced, to thine exalted strain!
I die! I die! but not for want of bliss—
But with the riches of my happiness!
I stagger underneath the heavy load
Of too much joy along this thorny road!

I sink down, weary, underneath the Cross
That leads to Heaven from earth where all is dross!
Oh! lift me out of this divine distress
Of happiness—this plenitude of bliss—
This Eden of Delights—this overflow
Of Heaven into my soul now laid so low
With its excessive splendors of delight—
This blinding of my soul with too much light!
This emptying of the sun upon my soul,
While over me his wheels of glory roll,
Pressing from out my heart Promethean tears—
Poured from the Cycles of his rhythmic years—
As if Eternity were into Time
Emptied—mountains on mountains heaped sublime—
Far out of sight, into the Empyreal heights
Of Heaven, where dwell the infinite delights
Of God—that Crown of crowns—around whose top
Gather the Angels—shining climax of all hope!—
Now, as the star-crowned Angel of the Night
Gives to the dying Day divine delight—
Folding him gently in her arms to rest,
In the soft Chambers of the dewy West;
So fold my soul in the odorous bud
Of thy sweet opening Rose of Womanhood,
That I may there, embowered in perfume, lie,
And feed forever on thy heavenly purity!

———◆———

CHORAL SONG OF THE TEMPERANCE LEGIONS.

Wave, banners! wave!
Out of God's HOLY MOUNTAIN,
For the lips of the brave
Who were mighty to save,
Bearing LIFE on its wave—
Flows the cool crystal fountain—

Wave, banners! wave!
Blow, trumpets! blow!
Tell to Zion's sweet Daughter
How we conquered the foe
In the valley below—
(He is lying there now—)
By the BEAUTIFUL WATER.
Blow, trumpets! blow!

Wave, banners! wave!
Fill the world with the story
Of the deeds of the brave
Who were mighty to save—
Sending Hell to his grave
On the GREEN FIELDS OF GLORY!
Wave, banners! wave!
Blow, trumpets! blow!
Clothe them all now in whiteness;
For the CHURCHES are so
Filling Earth with their snow,
That the Valley below
Looks like heaven in its brightness!
Blow, trumpets! blow!

VILLA ALLEGRA, Jan. 1, 1847.

THE POET OF LOVE.

The Poet of Love receives divine ovation
Not only from Angel's hands while here on earth;
But all the Ages echo back, with salutations,
The Trumpet of the Skies in praises on his worth;
And all the Islands of the Sea
Of the vast immensity.

Echo the music of the Morns,
Blown through the Corybantine Horns
Down the dark vistas of the reboantic Norns,＊
By the great Angel of Eternity,
Thundering, *Come to me! come to me!*

From the inflorescence of his own high soul,
　The incense of his Eden-song doth rise,
Whose golden river of pure redolence doth roll
　　Down the dark vistas of all time in melodies—
　　　Echoing the Islands of the Sea
　　　Of the vast immensity,
　　　And the loud music of the Morns,
　　　Blown through the Conchimarian Horns
　　　Down the dark vistas of the reboantic Norns,
　　　By the great Angel of Eternity,
　　　Thundering, *Come to me! come to me!*

With the white lightnings of his still small voice,
　Deep as the thunders of the azure Silence—
He makes dumb the oracular Cymbals with their noise,
　　Till BEAUTY flourish Amaranthine on the Islands
　　　Of all the loud tumultuous Sea
　　　Of the vast immensity,
　　　Echoing the music of the Morns,
　　　Blown through the Chrysomelian Horns,
　　　Down the dark vistas of the reboantic Norns,
　　　By the great Angel of Eternity,
　　　Thundering, COME TO ME! COME TO ME!

＊The three Maidens (Nornir) who dwell in one of the fair Cities of Heaven by the Spring of Urdar, under the boughs of the great tree Igdrasel, whose names are Udr, Verthandi and Skulld—Past, Present and Future. They are Liosalfar —that is, Light Alfs—and are brighter than the sun.

TO ADA IN PARADISE.

As fades the Violet in the dews of morning,
  Whose tender leaves should have revived therewith,
Didst thou, with rosy health thy cheeks adorning—
  Seming most deathless in the arms of Death!

As wakes the Violet Winter Frosts have withered,
  Putting on beauty new in Spring again—
Re-robed with fadeless splendor newly gathered—
  Shalt thou from Death to Life in Heaven to reign.

Blessed forever! blessed be thy springing
  From Death's cold Winter to immortal bloom,
As Dove-like thy pure soul to Heaven goes singing,
  Borne up by Angels from the silent tomb.

VILLA ALLEGRA, GA., Sept. 8, 1848.

———◆———

THE COMFORTER.

Clad in the armor of celestial love,
  Forevermore my soul with sorrow weepeth!
A "still small voice" comes down from Heaven above—
  "*Weep not, she is not dead, but sleepeth.*"

For when the Ruler's daughter lay in death—
  (So, for her only son the widow weepeth—)
Christ's love made answer to his fervent faith—
  "*Weep not, she is not dead, but sleepeth.*"

Like that poor widow at the gates of Nain,
  A father for his only son now weepeth!
But Christ's sweet voice is heard above the train—
  "WEEP NOT, HE IS NOT DEAD, BUT SLEEPETH."

1847

THE NEW MOON.

"Oh! gentle Moon!"—SHELLEY.

I see the infant pale New Moon,
    Just from the Old One born;
She had her birth this day at noon,
    And this is her first horn.

She lies now in the arms afar
    Of azure Heaven at rest;
While by her side the Evening Star
    Watches her in the West.

Like some sweet, heavenly dying Hymn,
    Pausing in going down—
She lingers on the horizon's rim
    A moment—now is gone!

MIDDLETOWN, CONN., October 18, 1840.

———◆———

SONG OF SALEM.

A FRAGMENT.

Waving their Banners high—
Snow-white Ensignia of the Reign of Peace—
    For which the LORD OF GLORY left to die
His Father's Salem—never more to cease—
They hail their great SHEKINAH, who arose
From Death, that Heaven might triumph o'er her foes!

Crying aloud, All hail!
Unto the Mighty! unto Him who reigns
    At the right hand of God in Heaven! prevail,
Ye Mighty Ones!   Jerusalem! thy stains
Are washed away! thou art as white as snow,
And shalt remain on earth forever so!

All hail! all hail! arise,
Ye Legatees of Endless Life! shake Heaven
   With clapping your white hands! he dies! he dies!
The Demon of the Earth! fierce Truth has riven
Him, as the Lightning rends the clouds, in twain—
Never to vex, with war, the earth again!

     Aloud, ye Sons of Men!
Rejoice! rejoice! the Reign of Peace is come!
   The SUN OF RIGHTEOUSNESS descends again,
With healing on his wings, to take us home—
The ransomed of his love—the righteous given
To enter joyful with their Lord in Heaven!

NEW YORK, April 10th, 1841.

———⸙———

SONNET TO ISA.

As some lone Nightingale, his mate within her nest,
   The whole night long in sweet, harmonious strains—
(Tending her young beneath her fostering breast—)
   Pledging his love, repays her for her pains,
And all those irksome duties she fulfills
   Of incubation—fills the silent woods
With music, sometimes softer than the rills—
   Then louder—gushing—till the solitudes
Are deluged with unfathomed song, which flows,
   Like incense from an Altar, all around,
As sweet as perfume from the trampled rose—
   Filling the bending heavens with odorous sound—
So does my soul as bounteous as the dew,
Pour out its gratitude in song for you!

MIDDLETOWN, CONN., April 10, 1839.

THE ANGELUS.

A wave-like, azure sound,
Upon the pavement of new-fallen snow,
  Pure as an Angel's garment on the ground—
Trembling the atmosphere with its soft flow—
Comes swiftly, with its Heaven-dilating swell,
From the Noon-ringing of yon far-off Bell.

  In billowy circles round,
In all directions from the trembling rim,
  Upon the sea-like atmosphere, the wave-like sound
Goes spreading, like the setting Moon grows dim—
As soft-embosomed in the air it lies
Waning away its soul until it dies.

  Into the azure grave
Of Silence, in the embrace of the sky,
  Now buried, lies the soft Æolian wave,
Lulled to repose by its own melody—
Soft as the down upon the Cygnet's breast,
Embayed, at noontide, in some lake at rest.

MIDDLETOWN, CONN., August 8, 1841.

------◈------

LIBERTY.

O, Nomen dulce libertatis!—CIC. AD VER.

When Truth's broad pinions scourged the angry Night
Which sepulchred the Nations, then the Earth,
Rejoicing in the splendor of her might,
Bade freedom from her mighty Tomb come forth!
As when an Earthquake, from his Dœdal Cave,
Rises aloft, stupendous, from the sleep
Of centuries—so rose she from her grave,
Making the Tyrant in her presence weep!

The sound, like thunder, broke on Europe's shore,
Where many millions bent the abject knee—
Crouching to hear the British Lion roar !
For when they heard the shout of LIBERTY !
They started !—an electric shiver ran,
Like lightning, through each vein—(as Ocean's waves
Beneath the Whirlwind's breath,) when, man by man,
They stood erect, forgetting they were slaves !
But like the blighted Forest in the storm,
Worm-eaten at the heart, by Whirlwinds slain—
Laden with heavy chains—each manly form
Fell prostrate—hushing in his broken heart
The earthquake of sweet joy, which therein sprung
As flowers from out the earth are seen to start—
Then die all suddenly, though they are young !
And though weighed down beneath the weight of chains,
Mildewed by their own tears, which fell thereon
In torrents, wrung from out their hearts, whose pains
Were agonies,—the name of WASHINGTON
Fell on their ears like dew upon parched flowers,
Greening their souls with joy—till they were free
From Tyranny's dark wings—(from all such powers,)
Whose shade is death—to dwell with LIBERTY !
Oh ! 'twas the sweetest sound ear ever heard !
A Voice whose music was the Soul of Love !
Known unto many only by that word—
For Angels bent to hear it from above !
If ever there was one foul name on earth,
It is that cruel, cursed name called King !
Beneath whose breath no freedom can come forth—
And in whose path no flowery good can spring !
He is that foul embodiment of wrong—
Injustice brooding over human right—
Who, in the absence of the TRUTH, grows strong,
But, in her presence, sinks to abject night !

10*

This Angel, brooding first upon the sea—
Whose mighty wings were spread from shore to shore—
Is soaring Westward now, whose flight shall be
A scourge to Darkness which flies on before—
Where Freedom's children, in the bands of love,
Crowned with the Oaky boughs forever green—
Shall feast with joy, while Angels from above
Shall smile in transport on the joyful scene—
And hear the scream of Eagles from the East,
Answering the scream of Eagles from the West,
Coming, their last time, from their final feast
Upon the flesh of Kings, in peace to rest.

1836.

----&----

THE BLOOD-STAINED ALDER.

A SONG OF FREEDOM FOR THE LYRE.

When the bright Sun of Freedom had set
    On poor Poland, the Land of the Brave!
And the soil that they fought for, was wet
    With the blood which they died but to save;
By the walls of great Warsaw there stood
    A young Alder Tree covered with gore,
Which their children dug up for the blood
    Which its green tender branches then bore.

A poor Exile, when seeking his rest
    In America, Land of the Free!
Set it out in the far, fertile West,
    Where it sprouted to Liberty's Tree.
For, when Prussia had triumphed, he kept
    The young Tree for the blood that it bore;
And, whenever he looked on it, wept
    For the Land he should visit no more!

Like that Exile of Poland, ye Sons
    Of the Mighty who died to be free !
Let each drop of the blood which now runs
    Through your veins, nourish Liberty's Tree !
For, as that was so dear to the Poles
    Because stained with their forefather's gore,
Let each relic be dear to our souls,
    Which our own have left us—evermore.

VILLA ALLEGRA, GA., June 8, 1846.

---◈---

THE EXILE'S LAMENT.

My early love, my early love,
    Thy music once was sweet !
But now, alas ! my early love,
    We never more shall meet !
Ah ! how my heart doth beat
    To see again my early love,
Whose music once was sweet ;
    But now, alas ! my early love,
We never more shall meet !

My early love, my early love,
    Thy soul can never know
The sod that hides thy wandering Dove
    In this wide world below !
Ah ! how my tears do flow,
To see again my early love,
    Whose soul can never know
The sod that hides her wandering Dove
    In this wide world below !
      Ah ! no, no, no—
    Can never, never know
The sod that hides her wandering Dove
    In this wide world below !

1830.

SONNET.

HARRISON.

In the serene evening of his bye-gone days,
The sun of righteousness shed on his brow
A holy light—more beautiful than now
Appears high Heaven—too beautiful for praise!
His goodness bankrupt leaves the mightiest tongue!
For, as Heaven's arch, at night, with black is hung,
With mourning is the Country of his fame!
While, star-like, through the gloom, appears his name
Making the darkness beautiful with rays
That melt our sorrow, as the burning light
Of Hesperus the darkness of the night—
Defying all Earth's combined powers to raze
One atom of his memory from mankind—
As well may they attempt to fetter mind.

NEW YORK, April 6, 1841.

CHAUNT OF HOPE.

Through the dark, selfish flesh-clouds that obscure
    Our dear Humanity's divinest morning,
God's golden Sun beams down serenely pure,
    Clothing our souls again with pure adorning.

Truth now descends upon us, like the Dove
    To Christ from Heaven, when unto Him was spoken
Those words of consolation from above—
    Pouring Heaven's oil into our hearts when broken!

Rich beauty, like the dewy flush of morn,
    Lives incarnated in the form of woman,
Our earthly Ideal of the Heavenly-Born—
    Our Heavenly living in the Angel-Human.

True love is born with an eternal youth,
    And brightest burns in darkest night of sorrow—
Pure as the Dove's divine connubial truth—
    Telling to-day what it will be to-morrow.

Her soft caressings fall with Dove-like peace
    Upon our thorny pillows, ever trying—
Bringing unto our souls that sweet release
    Which only Angels bring unto the dying.

1840.

---✦---

THE WIND.

Thou wringest, with thy invisible hand, the foam
    Out of the emerald drapery of the sea,
Beneath whose foldings lies the Sea-Nymph's* home—
    Lifted, to make it visible, by thee;
Till thou art exiled, earthward, from the maine,
To cool the parched tongue of the Earth with rain.

Thy viewless wing sweeps, with its tireless flight,
    Whole Navies from their boundings on the waves—
Wrapping the canvas, pregnant with thy might,
    Around the seamen in their watery graves!
Till thou dost fall asleep upon the grass,
And then the ocean is as smooth as glass.

Thou art the Gardner of the flowery earth—
    The Sower in the spring-time of the year—
Clearing plantations, in thy goings forth,
    Amid the wilderness, where all is drear—
Scattering ten thousand giant oaks around,
    Like playthings, on the dark, opprobrious ground.

NEW YORK, October. 10, 1839.

*The ancient writers peopled the sea with Nymphs, whom they called Nereids. See Homer's description of Thetis and the seagreen sisters weeping for the death of Patrocles. Camoens, the Portuguese Poet, speaks of them in the first book of his Lusiad.

THE NIGTINGALE OF HEAVEN.

Composed on hearing Madame Coradori Allen sing in the Arch Street Theatre, Philadelphia.

Sweet Nightingale of Heaven! thou art the Bird
    That in the groves of Nature poured her song,
Till the deep fountains of my soul were stirred,
    As never stirred before by mortal tongue!
And like the billows of the azure lake,
    Circling the beauty of the milky swan—
Curled by her bosom on the shore to break
    In liquid kisses as she circles on;
So, from thy bosom waves the liquid song
    Which spreads triumphantly my spirit o'er—
Bringing me healing, as it floats along,
    Like blessings from Eternity's bright shore.

1837.

HYMN FROM THE INNER LIFE.

How long before the bloody sweat of anguish,
    Bathing my marble brow, shall cease to flow?
Or cease my soul in this dark world to languish,
    Waiting for that which Earth can never know?
        This is the burden of my song—
        "How long, Oh! Lord! how long?"

How long before our souls, like ministering Angels,
    Shall do each other deeds of heavenly love,
By acting out the Lord's divine Evangels—
    Doing God's will on earth as it is done above?
        This is the burden of my song—
        "How long, Oh! Lord! how long?"

How long before the world shall know its duty—
   Man treat Man right—right take the place of wrong—
Truth, clad in garments of supernal beauty,
    Triumph o'er Error that has grown so strong ?
        Answer this burden of my song—
        " How long, Oh ! Lord ! how long ? "

Soon shall Man's soul be bathed in blissful wonder,
   Hearing Heaven's choral shouts burst through the sky—
God's Scripture rolling down in rhythmic thunder
   Out of the diapason of the stars on high.
        Then shall this burden of my song
        Be changed to joy as deep as life is long.

———◈———

VISION OF THE HEAVENLY ONES.

     'Twas in the flowery month of May,
     About the noontide hour of day,
     That two bright Angels, full of love,
     Came down to me from Heaven above,
     With golden harps within their hands,
     Made in the high Elysian Lands,
     Amid the Bowers of Asphodel,
     Where Angel-souls forever dwell—
     Bright golden harps with silver strings,
     Which they o'ershadowed with their wings,
     Outstretched above of snowy white,
     Now glinting back the golden light
     From God's high throne in Heaven above—
     The light of his eternal love—
     Which, striking, they now sang to me
     A song of joy incessantly—

A holy song of heavenly love,
Such as the Angels sing above—
Such as the Angels sing on high—
A song of immortality.
They were two infant Cherubim
Who sang to me that Heavenly Hymn.
One had the same cerulean eyes
Of my first-born now in the skies;
The other's eyes were dark, with light
Therein like Hesperus to the night—
Such as to my dear son were given,
The Image of that One from Heaven;
For my dear children had the eyes
Of those bright Angels from the skies—
The same as they appeared to me
Eight years before their infancy.
'Twas in the flowery month of May,
About the noontide hour of day,
And on the same day in the year
On which the Angels did appear,
Revealing joys which were, to me,
Prophetic of what was to be—
That tidings came to me what morn
ALLEGRA FLORENCE should be born;
And she was born—the very child
That came to me, the undefiled,
And played upon her harp that day,
All in the flowery month of May.
How beautiful, divine, thou wert,
Thus issuing from thy mother's heart,
Singing, most piteously, to me
The first song of thine infancy.
She was my Salem from her birth—
My young Jerusalem on earth—
Allegra Florence with blue eyes,
Who, at the gate of Paradise,

Now stands, all purified from sin,
Waiting to let her father in
The Old Jerusalem above—
The Holy Land of Heavenly Love.

———❖———

TRUST IN GOD.

I see the deep blue sky above—
  Below the dark blue sea;
The first, the image of God's love—
  The last—Eternity!

Oh! as the deep blue sky above
  Upon this dark blue sea,
Does God, in his calm, happy love,
  Look down from Heaven on me.

On the Ocean, July 10, 1837.

———❖———

TO CARIE.

" Je ne vois rein que mecontente
Absent de ma Divinite."—M. Noailes to the Princess de Conde.

Dear Carie! I am all alone,
  With no one, now, to comfort me!
The snow-white Dove of Joy has flown
  Out of my heart in losing thee!

The Violets reappear in Spring—
  The young dove with the new-born year;
But when wilt thou return to bring
  Back to my soul all these, my dear?

The grief that once in thee was lost,
  Returns again to make me pine;
Because the Joy my heart loved most,
  Remains away along with thine!

11

SONNET

ON READING MRS. BROWNING'S DRAMA OF EXILE.

Like some great storm-cloud from the troubled ocean,
Pregnant with lightnings which are born in thunder,
Waxing like mountains in their Heaven-ward motion,
Till, by their own strength, they are torn asunder—
Weeping themselves to death in freshning rain;
So rose up from thy soul that God-like strain,
In Miriam-jubilations through the sky,
Filling the star-gemmed altitudes on high
With deep, pathetic wailings, full of pain!
Then, like Apolyon's last sigh, when he fell,
Scented with memories of his Eden-gladness—
God's mercy following him with wrath to Hell—
While Angels' tears drop on him in their sadness;
So died upon my soul thy song in blissful madness.

OAK GROVE, GA., September 10, 1845.

TO AN ANGEL ON EARTH.

"Spouse! sister! Angel!"—SHELLEY.

The moment that mine eyes were fixed on thee,
    I knew that Heaven ordained thee to be mine;
And felt how happy this fond heart would be,
    Were it but only to be twinned with thine.

My soul was so enamored then of thee,
    I knew no other boon than thou hadst given;
For thy surpassing beauty was to me
    The first of my forgetfulness of Heaven.

Oh! if our souls would only swear to dwell
    Twin-mated in this world, to live or die;
Mine would be happier, loving thine so well,
    Than are the Angels in the Heavens on high.

NEW YORK, June 10, 1840.

SONNET.

THE SONGS OF BIRDS.

" The songs of birds, and the life of Man, are both brief, both soul-filled, and both, as they end, leave behind whispers
of Heaven."—JEAN PAUL RICHTER.

The Angel-spirits of all men are glad
At the sweet singing of the joyful birds—
For they have more intelligence than words,
And are best comforts to the heart when sad.
The afflicted, journeying here on earth. are made
More joyful by these Minstrels of the grove,
Whose songs are waftings of the soul of love,
Breathed from Affection's fountain—they are clad
In tones like hues in which they are arrayed—
Some scarlet—others azure—such the Dove,
Whose song is like the soul's love-breathing sigh,
As if an inspiration from above
Had kindled in its heart one melody,
The breath of which is love that cannot die.

NEW YORK, May 23, 1841.

———◈———

UNE SONGE D'UNE NUIT D'ETE.

Come, sing the sweet song that you sang unto me,
    When the hopes of my soul were so bright—
When you smiled on my heart as the Moon on the Sea—
    Called *The Song of the Sweet Summer Night.*
Come, sing it, sweet lady! oh! sing it again,
    That my soul may be rapt with delight—
Shedding peace on her heart as the Moon on the Maine
    When she comes on some sweet Summer Night.

You know the sweet song that you sang in the Bower,
    When the Nightingale warbled all night,
Till the perfumes were pressed from each new opening flower
    By his heart, that throbbed wild with delight?

Oh ! sing it, sweet lady ! *do* sing it again,
   That my soul may be rapt with delight—
Shedding peace on my heart as the Moon calms the Maine,
   When she comes on some sweet Summer Night.

Come, sing the sweet song that you once sang to me,
   On the Halcyon Sea of Delight—
When my soul on the waves of thy voice floated free—
   Called *The Song of the Sweet Summer Night.*
Oh ! sing it, sweet lady ! *do* sing it again,
   That the hopes of my soul may be bright—
It will calm me to peace as the Moon calms the Maine—
   Called *The Song of the Sweet Summer Night.*

TONTINE HOTEL, July 4, 1852.

----✤----

LAMORAH'S DEATH SONG FOR HIS SON.

No, pale-face ! thou shalt expect the tears
   That the father sheds for his dying son !
But the spring dries up after many years—
   And from these old eyes there shall fall not one !
I have heard thee say that my death was nigh !
That my tribe must fall ! that my son shall die !
I can only say for my warrior-love,
Oh ! white-man ! slay not my eagle-dove !

The few short years you may rob from me,
   Will pass like the winds on the raging floods ;
But the sudden fall of my son shall be
   Like the mighty oak in the silent woods ! ✻
If the bitterest death that my life can give,
Be enough for his—let the young boy live !
If, by burning up, I can save my love—
Oh ! white-man ! slay not my eagle-dove !

✻ Nearly a verbatim expression of Pushmataha.

I know not why that his early death
    Should deter my tale—for the deed was done!
I was once along on this very path,
    And perceived three babes in the woods alone!
I threw them up in the air for life,
And caught them all on my pointed knife—
The knife that now would avenge my love—
Oh! white-man! slay not my eagle-dove!

The turtle hies to his cedar-nest,
    And the roebuck wanders from hill to hill;
And the eagle ascends to the sun to rest—
    But the same deep pangs are my portion still;
For the valley-path where the infants smiled,
And the awful look of that dying child—
Are upon me still—on my warrior-love—
Oh! white-man! slay not my eagle-dove!

Oh! think not, man! that my heart is free
    From the iron cares that corrode the breast;
I am fastened here, like an inland sea,
    By the stagnant waves of my woes opprest!
I have not *one* hope that my tongue can tell!
I have only felt that my soul is—Hell!
I can only feel for my warrior-love—
Oh! white-man! slay not my eagle-dove!

CHEROKEE NATION, March 10, 1831.

------♦------

TO AN ANGEL IN HEAVEN.

"Il vago spirito ardente
E'en alto intelletto, un puro core."—PETRARCH.

I worshipped thee, in thy bright perfectness, afar,
    As Chaldea's sons the brightest star of even;
And longed, as they, to be with my bright star,
    Because, like theirs, thou wert so nigh to Heaven.

I knew to worship thee was to adore
 That Being who had made thee so divine;
And felt my heart grow happier than before,
 By only wishing it to be with thine.

I felt, while gazing on thy beauteous face,
 And the calm languor of those dove-like eyes,
And that angelic form of Heavenly grace—
 That thou wert sure an angel in disguise.

I saw my soul to gaze on thee was lost,
 Though, in thy presence, it grew more divine;
For, when my spirit wanted thee the most,
 I knew, alas! thou never couldst be mine!

And thus, while gazing on thy loveliness,
 The night itself grew more like day to me;
For, in thy smiles the earth like earth grew less,
 And more like Heaven—when Heaven to Heaven took thee!
1830.

TO MY LITTLE DAUGHTER.

A PARAPHRASE.

Jehovah is my Shepherd! He will feed
My little Florence in her hour of need:
He maketh her sweet soul, in Heaven's high noon,
Beside the LIVING WATERS, to lie down:
He will restore her soul when it is faint,
And never suffer her to be in want:
For he will raise her from the grave beneath,
And lead her safely through the Vale of Death;
And comfort her, if she should feel distress,
And smile forever on her loveliness.
1842.

SONNET.

GRIEF.

" Sorrow is better than laughter; for by the sadness of the countenance the heart is made better."—BIBLE.

As the uncertain twittering of the birds,
    Striving with Winter, which has been so long,
Dies inarticulate—ending not in song—
    So did my voice, with many plaintive words,
Strive, in the winter of my grief, to sing,
    But died in silence—they could not be spoken—
Because, within my heart, there was no spring
    Of joy to call them forth—*my heart was broken!*
For Disappointment's frost had withered up
    Affection's flowers!—Youth's Garden now was bare!
I have drunk poison from Death's empty cup,
    Whose bottom now contains the dregs of care,
Which mock my lips with bitterness, to think
    That of Youth's wine there is no more to drink!

NEW YORK, May 23, 1841.

---❖---

THE SONG OF SERALIM.

A CELESTIAL MELOLOGUE.

"Break forth into joy, sing."—ISAIAH.

RAPHAEL.

The Stars are pausing in their orbs to-night,
    And silence is the concert which they hymn;
For they are rapt to dumbness with delight
    Listening to hear the song of SERALIM!

GABRIEL.

Myriads of Angels are assembled near,
    Clad in white garments, whiter than pure snow,
From all Heaven's flowery realms afar to hear
    Oceans of music from his sweet lips flow.

MICHAEL.

For, as the Stars drink glory from the Sun,
   And without which they soon would cease to shine—
So do the Angels from that HOLY ONE
   In Heaven draw theirs, which makes them so divine.

CHORUS OF ANGELS IN HEAVEN.

From thy celestial lyre,
    O! SERALIM!
Scatter through Heaven the radiant notes of fire!
   And from thy soul-uplifting tongue,
In concert with each golden wire,
   Pour forth the living tide of song—
    The sweetest, holiest hymn
    That ever Angel sung!

SERALIM SINGS.

Praise God, ye Angels of the Heavens above!
   Praise Him, ye Seraphs who can never die!
And you, Archangels! whose delight is love,
   Thunder your anthems through eternity!

Let the uncounted Realms of endless Space
   Join in their orbits to unite in praise—
(Whose light is the reflection of His face—)
   Loving aloud the ANCIENT ONE OF DAYS!

Lift up your voices, Children of the Earth!
   Praise God, ye Spirits of the countless spheres!
And you, ye HABITANTS OF HEAVEN! pour forth
   The tide of song through Heaven's eternal years!

Fill up the canopy of Heaven above
   With song's immortal, everlasting sea;
And drown the Stars in one wide sea of love
   Poured forth in praises to the Deity.

CHORUS OF ANGELS IN HEAVEN.

Above all that Archangel ever taught,
  Rapt in the highest bliss of Heaven divine—
Second alone to Him the CAUSE of thought—
  O! SERALIM! was that sweet song of thine!

OAK GROVE, GA., 1836.

CONSOLATION.

"I will sing unto the Lord as long as I live."—DAVID.

Shout, ye Redeemed! with one accordant voice!
Proclaim the victory over Death—rejoice!
Th' illustrious triumph over Sin prolong
In rapturous strains—the burden of our song!

Soon shall the hallowed carnival begin
Of Zion—everlasting—ushering in
The Sabbath of sweet rest unto the good,
When all of Moab's sons shall be subdued.

Star-crowns of glory shall adorn each head
Of those now resurrected from the dead;
But round the head of him who shunned the light,
A crown of darkness woven out of night!

This is the Anastasis we shall have—
A spiritual, glorious life beyond the grave—
Wearing the robes of glory Christ put on
Beneath the Rainbow of his Father's throne.

The lowering clouds that hung about the grave,
Were melted by the SON that came to save—
When, folding back the Vail that hid the light,
God's glory burst upon his raptured sight.

For, when his body from the grave came forth,
Then was the MAN-CHILD born upon the earth—
Then God proclaimed from Heaven's Eternity,
" This DAY, my SON ! have I begotten thee ! "

With reconciled expectancy we wait
To hail the opening of the Heavenly Gate
Of HIEROSOLYMA—celestial—bright—
At the Christ-couching of our mortal sight.

For, as God's voice broke through eternity,
Making the universe of worlds to be ;
So did this SPIRITUAL SAMPSON, without hands,
Tear up Hell's iron gates at his commands !

Thus the Believer on his dying bed,
When Death's dark night is lowering round his head ;
Draws round his faith the curtain of sweet calm,
In beatific vision of the LAMB.

1846.

————✥————

TO ENDEA.

" Her sins, which are many, are forgiven; for she loved much."—LUKE 7, 47.

If Mary's sins, because she " *loved so much*,"
    By ONE, who loved her more, were all forgiven ;
I know, sweet Endea ! that *our* love is such
    That we shall both be *sure* to go to Heaven.

For, if for " *loving much*," we are to win
    Approval of his love—*we are forgiven ;*
For we have loved enough to make our sin
    As white as snow before it falls from Heaven.

And if, like Mary, we should be accused
   Of equal crime, we shall be *still* forgiven;
For we shall err, however much abused,
   As " GOD IS LOVE "—upon the side of Heaven.

CONNECTICUT RIVER, August 3, 1839.

————❧————

CANZONET TO CARIE.

'Twas not within the lighted Hall,
   Where fashion gaily shone;
Nor was it at some Festival,
   Where beauty reigned alone;
But far off from the scenes of pride,
   That thou wert dear to me;
I gladly turned from all beside,
    And gave my soul to thee—
    To thee—alone to thee!
I gladly turned from all beside,
    And gave my soul to thee.

I sought thee not amid the throng,
   Where joy was wont to reign;
And seeking thee—though sought so long—
   I sought thee not in vain;
And now that nought can e'er divide
   Thy loveliness from me;
I gladly turn from all beside,
    And give my soul to thee—
    To thee—alone to thee!
I gladly turn from all beside,
    And give my soul to thee.

And now that thy dear voice is heard
  In eloquence and love;
And that our vows are registered
  By holy hands above;
And that thou art mine own soul's bride,
  And shalt forever be;
I gladly turn from all beside,
  And give my soul to thee—
  To thee—alone to thee!
I gladly turn from all beside,
  And give my soul to thee.

NEW YORK, November 20, 1837.

———◆———

CRADLE-SONG.

As the Dove, with her lily-white wings,
  Overshadows her young in her nest;
So, thy mother will watch while she sings,
  To her beautiful babe on her breast.
Thy sisters, that once were so bright,
  Are now gone to their home in the sky;
And thy father is watching to-night,
  For fear that his Emma may die.
Then sleep, little Emma, my pretty baby dear!
Thou fairest of babes ever born!
Thy father, who loves thee, is watching thee near,
  And will watch thee all night till the morn.
    When thy mother is nigh,
    She will sing *Isu-bye;* *
    And when she is away,
    I will sing, all the day,
      Lullaby! lullaby!

* Jesus be with you.

The Angels are whispering her now !
　　See ! see how she smiles in her sleep !
Be silent ! or speak to her low—
　　For fear you may make her to weep !
Oh ! guard her, ye Angels above !
　　Protect her, awake or asleep !
For the sake of her father's dear love,
　　Which keeps him awake now to weep !
Then sleep, little Emma, my pretty baby dear !
　　Thou fairest of babes ever born !
Thy father, who loves thee, is watching thee near,
　　And will watch thee all night till the morn.
　　　　When thy mother is nigh,
　　　　She will sing *Isu-bye ;*
　　　　And when she is away,
　　　　I will sing, all the day,
　　　　　Lullaby ! lullaby !

———✦———

ASTARTE'S SONG TO ENDYMION.

Come to thy Home in the Heavens above—
To the Flowery Land of the peaceful love—
To the Goshen-Isles where there is no night—
To the Golden Groves of the pure delight ;
For the Angels shall strew thy path with flowers,
And carry thee up through the Amaranth Bowers !
　　　Then come, oh ! quickly come !
　　　And rejoice in thy heavenly Home !

Come through the Valley of Death's dark shade,
All under the graves of the early dead !
Fording that Beautiful River whose flow
Is softer than sleep in the Vale below ;

For the night that falls on thy weary way,
Is the Night that leads to Eternal Day !
    Then come, oh ! quickly come !
    And rejoice in thy heavenly Home !

Come where the sorrows of Earth shall cease,
Where the Valley lies of Eternal Peace—
Watered by streams that are full of song,
Singing of God as they flow along—
Whose banks are as green with Eternal Spring
As the Bowers of Bliss where the Angels sing !
    Then come, oh ! quickly come !
    And rejoice in thy heavenly Home !

Come where thy tears shall be all wiped dry
By the hands of God—never more to die !
Where the songs of Angels shall never cease,
In that Beautiful Land of Eternal Peace—
To the Bowers of Bliss, where the friends of youth
All renew their vows of eternal truth !
    Then come—oh ! quickly come !
    And see God in thy heavenly Home !

Come to Astarte, who loves thee best,
And recline once more on her peaceful breast—
Wandering alone through the flowery Meads,
In the silver Vales of the sighing Reeds,
By the Living Streams, in the Violet Skies—
And re-sun thy soul in her beautiful eyes !
    Now come ! oh ! quickly come !
    And rejoice in thy heavenly Home !

VILLA ALLEGRA, GA., May 5, 1896.

SONNET.

THE HYPOCRITE.

Ye ask me in your senselessness of heart—
"Why do you weep? what you have lost, we lose!
From Adam down all men have felt the smart
Of parting from their mothers—which you choose
To dwell upon so long, as if to part
From yours was more than *ours* to part from those
That *we* love best! We all have felt the dart
Enter our souls!—*we*, too, have felt *thy* woes!"
Peace, heartless wretch! ye know not of the throes
Your senselessness hath caused!—ye have no art
Even to conceal your want of that which knows
In me no bounds—which ye have caused to start
Anew, in *pity* for thee, from repose!

NEW YORK, March 8, 1841.

SPRING.

"Tempus adest cantus avium;
Et vox turturis in terra nostra auditer."—SOLOMON'S SONGS.

Thy glorious smile, oh! Spring!
Is Earth's rejuvenation! every grove
And forest—every bird upon the wing—
The smiling Vales below—the Heavens above—
And every cloud that slumbers in the sky—
Even God himself—are glad that thou art nigh.

Thy genial influence
Pervades all things with life-imparting power!
Thou art the Season of the soul's deep sense
Of all that is most beautiful! Each flower,
By thee on Nature's page now written, is
A word by which the soul tells of its bliss.

IN THE WOODS, IN CONNECTICUT, April 1, 1841.

THE POET'S FAREWELL TO HIS HARP.

Farewell, Harp! oh! fare-thee-well!
  Thou hast been my solace ever,
And thy dear kind notes shall dwell
  In my bosom's home forever—
      Fare-thee-well!
Thou hast soothed me o'er the Mountains—
  Thou hast saved me by the Sea;
Thou hast filled me when the Fountains
  All were dry—farewell to thee!

Farewell, Harp! oh! fare-thee-well!
  Now thy silver chords are broken!
Though my soul doth love thee well,
  All my vows are quickly spoken—
      Fare-thee-well!
Thou hast soothed me o'er the Mountains—
  Thou hast saved me by the Sea;
Thou hast filled me when the Fountains
  All were dry—farewell to thee!

The Romantic Tradition in American Literature

An Arno Press Collection

Alcott, A. Bronson, editor. **Conversations with Children on the Gospels.** Boston, 1836/1837. Two volumes in one.

Bartol, C[yrus] A. **Discourses on the Christian Spirit and Life.** 2nd edition. Boston, 1850.

Boker, George H[enry]. **Poems of the War.** Boston, 1864.

Brooks, Charles T. **Poems, Original and Translated.** Selected and edited by W. P. Andrews. Boston, 1885.

Brownell, Henry Howard. **War-Lyrics** and Other Poems. Boston, 1866.

Brownson, O[restes] A. **Essays and Reviews Chiefly on Theology, Politics, and Socialism.** New York, 1852.

Channing, [William] Ellery (The Younger). **Poems.** Boston, 1843.

Channing, [William] Ellery (The Younger). **Poems of Sixty-Five Years.** Edited by F. B. Sanborn. Philadelphia and Concord, 1902.

Chivers, Thomas Holley. **Eonchs of Ruby:** A Gift of Love. New York, 1851.

Chivers, Thomas Holley. **Virginalia;** or, Songs of My Summer Nights. (Reprinted from *Research Classics,* No. 2, 1942). Philadelphia, 1853.

Cooke, Philip Pendleton. **Froissart Ballads,** and Other Poems. Philadelphia, 1847.

Cranch, Christopher Pearse. **The Bird and the Bell,** with Other Poems. Boston, 1875.

[Dall], Caroline W. Healey, editor. **Margaret and Her Friends.** Boston, 1895.

[D'Arusmont], Frances Wright. **A Few Days in Athens.** Boston, 1850.

Everett, Edward. **Orations and Speeches,** on Various Occasions. Boston, 1836.

Holland, J[osiah] G[ilbert]. **The Marble Prophecy,** and Other Poems. New York, 1872.

Huntington, William Reed. **Sonnets and a Dream.** Jamaica, N. Y., 1899.

Jackson, Helen [Hunt]. **Poems.** Boston, 1892.

Miller, Joaquin (Cincinnatus Hiner Miller). **The Complete Poetical Works of Joaquin Miller.** San Francisco, 1897.

Parker, Theodore. **A Discourse of Matters Pertaining to Religion.** Boston, 1842.

Pinkney, Edward C. **Poems.** Baltimore, 1838.

Reed, Sampson. **Observations on the Growth of the Mind.** *Including,* **Genius** (Reprinted from *Aesthetic Papers,* Boston, 1849). 5th edition. Boston, 1859.

Sill, Edward Rowland. **The Poetical Works of Edward Rowland Sill.** Boston and New York, 1906.

Simms, William Gilmore. **Poems:** Descriptive, Dramatic, Legendary and Contemplative. New York, 1853. Two volumes in one.

Simms, William Gilmore, editor. **War Poetry of the South.** New York, 1866.

Stickney, Trumbull. **The Poems of Trumbull Stickney.** Boston and New York, 1905.

Timrod, Henry. **The Poems of Henry Timrod.** Edited by Paul H. Hayne. New York, 1873.

Trowbridge, John Townsend. **The Poetical Works of John Townsend Trowbridge.** Boston and New York, 1903.

Very, Jones. **Essays and Poems.** [Edited by R. W. Emerson]. Boston, 1839.

Very, Jones. **Poems and Essays.** Boston and New York, 1886.

White, Richard Grant, editor. **Poetry:** Lyrical, Narrative, and Satirical of the Civil War. New York, 1866.

Wilde, Richard Henry. **Hesperia:** A Poem. Edited by His Son (William Wilde). Boston, 1867.

Willis, Nathaniel Parker. **The Poems, Sacred, Passionate, and Humorous, of Nathaniel Parker Willis.** New York, 1868.